PRAISE FOR JEREMY .

A clear, practical blueprint for turning AI into steady, diversified income—without the hype.

DR. LENA HARTMAN, AI STRATEGY ADVISOR

AND VISITING SCHOLAR

This guide translates complex automation concepts into actionable steps that even non-tech readers can implement today to start earning while they sleep.

RAJIV MENON, FOUNDER AND CEO OF AI

WEALTH LABS

Rooted in ethical, sustainable practices, it reveals how to build resilient income streams that scale over time.

CAMILA ORTIZ, SENIOR FELLOW, CENTER FOR

RESPONSIBLE TECHNOLOGY

HOW TO MAKE PASSIVE INCOME WITH AI AUTOMATION

HOW TO MAKE PASSIVE INCOME WITH AI AUTOMATION

CREATE SCALABLE PASSIVE INCOME WITH AI
AUTOMATION FOR NON-TECHNICAL BEGINNERS

THE AI WEALTH BUILDERS SERIES
BOOK 1

JEREMY SWAIN

BOOK BOUND STUDIOS

First Edition

To my family, whose unwavering support kept the flame alive. To the mentors and readers who believed in this path—may these pages help you build ethical, sustainable income with AI.

The future is already here — it's just not evenly distributed.

CONTENTS

EARNING WHILE YOU SLEEP (WITHOUT THE HYPE)

WHAT PASSIVE INCOME REALLY MEANS

Passive income is a phrase that gets thrown around a lot, but it's easy to misunderstand. At its core, passive income means you create something of value upfront and then it continues to generate earnings with little ongoing day-to-day effort. It's not a magic switch that turns off your work entirely. Instead, it's a carefully designed system that once set in motion, can keep producing returns while you focus on other things. Think of it as building a rounded engine, not lighting a single fire.

To be realistic, there are three types of income you'll hear about: active income, leveraged income, and what most people mean by passive income. Active income is straightforward: you exchange time for money in real time. If you stop, the money stops. Leveraged income sits somewhere between: you use tools, teams, or services to extend your impact beyond every hour you work. It's not purely passive, but the right leverage can dramatically reduce your personal hours. True passive income, the kind this book focuses on, relies on a well-designed system. It requires an upfront investment of time, learning, and sometimes capital, followed by maintenance that's manageable rather than consuming every waking hour.

The traps are real. People chase the dream of instant riches or perpetual, effortless cash flow. The reality is more modest—and more sustainable. A successful passive income stream often starts as something you can explain in a sentence and maintain with a few focused checks each week. It's not about one big launch that pays forever. It's about recurring value: a product, a service, or a process that an audience finds useful and is willing to pay for again and again. When you measure it this way, "earning while you sleep" isn't magic. It's a carefully constructed habit of design, testing, and refinement.

In this book, you'll see passive income framed as a port-folio of AI-powered systems. Each system has three common ingredients: a clear value proposition for a real audience, a repeatable process that delivers that value, and a reliable pathway for customers to discover and buy from you. AI helps you automate the heavy lifting—creating content, handling routine tasks, gathering insights, and even launching simple products. The key distinction you'll see echoed throughout is that automation reduces the amount of manual work required, but it does not remove the need for intention, ethics, and ongoing care.

WHY AI IS A GAME-CHANGER FOR NON-TECH PEOPLE

Artificial intelligence has shifted the barrier to entry for building income-generating systems. It's not just about flashy demos or sci-fi promises; it's about practical tools that you can use with minimal technical background. The word AI has become a broad umbrella that covers language models, image generators, data analyzers, automation scripts, and decision-making helpers. What changes the game for non-tech people is that you can lean on these tools to perform tasks that used to require specialized knowledge or a team.

Imagine you want a steady stream of helpful blog posts for a niche site. In the past, you'd either write them yourself, hire a writer, or outsource the work in scattered ways. Today, you can draft topics with an AI assistant, refine the drafts with a human touch, and set up a simple publishing workflow that updates automatically. You can compile newsletters that feel personal but run on a predictable cadence, using AI to brainstorm ideas, draft sections, and curate relevant links. You can also automate routine customer inquiries with chatbots, tool recommendations, or suppressed emails that run on time.

The practical upside is not just speed; it's consistency and scale. AI helps you turn a handful of ideas into a machine that produces value repeatedly. You still need to design for your audience, maintain quality, and respect ethical boundaries. AI can generate content, data insights, or product ideas, but it won't magically know what your audience wants unless you provide the human context. The best outcomes come when you pair your domain knowledge or passions with AI's ability to process and organize information.

One mental model helps here. See AI as an assistant that handles repetitive or data-heavy tasks with a level of precision and speed you could not achieve alone. Your job is to frame problems as solvable questions, set guardrails for quality and safety, and then guide the output toward practical, human-ready results. As you navigate this book, you'll build a toolkit that blends your everyday skills with AI's capabilities. This is not about pretending you're a tech genius. It's about designing systems that work for you, 24/7, even when you're not actively coding or writing or consulting.

Ethics and responsibility aren't optional. The simplest way to think about it is to treat AI-assisted work the way you'd treat any business decision with real people involved: with honesty about what you deliver, transparency about your methods, and a commitment to do no harm. If you keep that compass, AI becomes a powerful enabler rather than a shortcut that derails trust.

WHO THIS BOOK IS FOR (ROLES, GOALS, AND STARTING POINTS)

This book is written for people at different points in their careers, with different goals—but a shared interest in earning more by doing less, or by doing what matters more efficiently. If you're an employee who wants to supplement your income without taking on another full-time job, you'll find a path that fits into evenings, weekends, or a few concentrated hours during the week. If you're a freelancer or consultant who feels the grind of chasing new clients or trading hours for dollars, you'll see how to productize parts of your expertise into scalable offerings supported by AI tools. If you're a solopreneur or creator who wants to reach more people without burning out, you'll learn how to design content and products that sustain themselves and grow over time. If you're a small online business owner, you'll discover ways to automate back-office operations, customer service, and marketing so the business runs more smoothly and your time becomes a strategic asset rather than a bottleneck. If you're new to AI, and non-technical by background, you'll find approachable explanations and practical steps that don't require you to become a coder.

People come with different starting points, but the thread that ties them together is a desire to build something that works beyond a single season or a single campaign. Some readers have a little spare capital to invest in tools or templates. Others have more time but less money to spare. A few have the luxury of both but lack technical confidence. Wherever you stand, the book offers a path that respects your situation rather than ignores it. The key is to match your goals with your current skills and to view AI as a way to unlock what you already know and care about.

If your goal is to create a replicable model you can improve over time, you're in the right place. If your goal is simply to automate a tedious task you hate, you'll still find value, but the journey will be about turning that start into something more durable. The most important starting point is honesty about where you are right now and what you're willing to learn. This book meets you there with practical, beginner-friendly guidance that honors your time and your growth."},{

WHAT YOU'LL BUILD: AI-POWERED INCOME SYSTEMS, NOT INSTANT RICHES

Here is where the conversation moves from promise to practice. You will not wake up tomorrow with a full portfolio of effortless income. What you will build, starting today, is a suite of AI-powered systems that deliver value to real people in real markets. Each system is designed to be repeatable, scalable, and capable of running with only occasional check-ins. The goal is to shift from trading hours for money to building processes that accumulate impact and revenue over time.

A typical system begins with a clear purpose: a problem you know people want solved. It would be paired with a reliable method for delivering that solution—content, data insights, a digital product, or a service—and with a mechanism for customers to discover and buy it. AI accelerates the cycle by generating content, analytics, and drafts, and by guiding decisions with patterns drawn from the data you collect. The result is a loop that can continue with minimal day-to-day input.

Think of a few concrete examples that you might build as you move through the book. One system could be a blog or niche site that uses AI to produce a steady stream of beginner-friendly posts, a newsletter that shares curated insights, and an evergreen product or mini course that complements the content. Another system might be an automated service offering—productized consulting where AI handles the operational backbone, while you provide the strategic oversight and client relationship management. A third system could be a digital asset library or a toolkit that you repeatedly update and sell with minimal incremental effort. Each of these has the potential to become a small, durable revenue stream when designed with audience needs in mind and built on reliable processes.

There are two guardrails you should keep in mind as you proceed. First, your income system is built to last, not to collapse at the first signs of volatility. That means choosing problems with persistent demand and avoiding fads that rely on one-off trends. Second, the quality of the output matters as much as the quantity. AI can flood you with ideas or drafts, but you will need to curate, refine, and test to ensure your product or service remains useful and trustworthy. The most successful systems are those that blend AI efficiency with human judgment, empathy, and accountability.

The path to building these systems is not a sprint, but a series of deliberate, incremental steps. You'll break down a project into manageable modules, set up the automation once, then monitor it and improve it over time. The payoff is not instant, but it is durable: recurring revenue, more free time, and a sense of control over how you spend your days. As you practice, you'll start identifying which activities naturally scale for you and which parts you still want to keep hands-on. It's about choosing the right balance and letting the systems carry the weight where they make the most sense.

Throughout the book you'll encounter a framework for evaluating opportunities, selecting the right tools, and validating ideas before you invest heavily in them. This is not about chasing every shiny object. It's about picking a few high-leverage opportunities, proving they work, and then expanding them through repeatable processes. You'll finish this chapter with a clear sense of what your first AI-powered income system could look like and a realistic plan to bring it to life.

HOW TO USE THIS BOOK: ROADMAP, EXERCISES, AND SUGGESTED READING PATH

This book is designed as a practical companion, not a theoretical manifesto. You'll move through it by following a simple rhythm: learn the concept, see how it applies in a real-world example, and then apply what you've learned with small, doable exercises. The exercises aren't busy-work; they're focused prompts that help you articulate your value proposition, sketch a workflow, test a small piece of automation, or validate a market need. They're intentionally brief so you can fit them into a busy day, yet they're designed to push you toward tangible results.

The roadmap is built around practical chapters that incrementally raise your capability. You'll start with the foundations, then move toward opportunity discovery and the toolset, followed by content engines, productized offers, and automated operations. By the time you reach the mid-section of the book, you'll be ready to design and launch your first AI-powered system. The later chapters are about refining, scaling, and sustaining your momentum, with a clear emphasis on ethics, risk management, and staying adaptable in a rapidly changing landscape.

To get the most from this book, treat it as a hands-on guide. Read a section, then pause to map your current situation—your time, your resources, and your goals. Use the exercises as checkpoints and validation gates. If you're time-pressed, you can skim the early chapters to build a framework and then return for the hands-on sections when you're ready to take action. The book also includes suggested reading paths designed to accommodate different starting points. If you're brand new to AI, begin with the foundations and a gentle overview of how AI actually works in day-to-day workflows. If you already have some technical or business experience, you can jump more quickly into opportunity discovery and tool selection, using the guiding questions in each section to tailor your approach.

Finally, ethics and sustainability run through every chapter. The book invites you to consider not only what you can automate, but what you should automate, how your work affects others, and how to protect your reputation in a world where automation can blur lines. The suggested path is not a rigid blueprint but a flexible plan you can adapt. Your goal is to leave this book with a practical, personalized roadmap—one that respects your time, supports your goals, and keeps you moving toward a life where you can earn, learn, and grow—even while you sleep.

ONE

FOUNDATIONS – UNDERSTANDING AI, AUTOMATION, AND ONLINE INCOME

AI IN PLAIN ENGLISH: WHAT IT IS AND WHAT IT CAN DO FOR YOU

Imagine a tireless assistant who can read, write, summarize, and organize information at speeds no human can match. That is a practical way to picture *artificial intelligence* in today's world. At its core, AI is a set of tools that understand language, analyze patterns, and generate useful outputs based on what you tell it to do. A lot of AI you've probably already interacted with lives in your everyday digital life—spell checkers that suggest corrections, email filters that sort messages into folders, search engines that guess what you want to find, and chat features that respond when you type a question. These are all small but real examples of AI at work. When we talk about AI in the context of making money online, we're focusing on how these capabilities can automate parts of your work, help you scale, and free up time for the things only you can do well.

One practical way to visualize AI is to think in terms of two big capabilities: language understanding and automation. Language models, the engines behind much of the AI you hear about, are trained on vast amounts of text. They learn patterns for how people write, what information tends to follow what, and how to adapt tone to different audiences. The magic happens when you give them a prompt—an instruction or a goal—and they produce a usable result. They can draft blog outlines, rewrite product descriptions to be more compelling, translate simple content into another language, or summarize a long article into a few key takeaways. In other words, they help you transform ideas into action more quickly, with less manual drafting and editing time.

Automation, on the other hand, is about turning repeated tasks into repeatable processes. It's not just about a single tool doing a one-off job; it's about connecting tools so one action triggers another. For example, a newsletter work-flow can start with an AI-generated topic idea, move to an outline draft, then to a full article, and finally to a social media post schedule—all without you manually tweaking every step. The end result is not magic; it is an engineered sequence of actions designed to produce a predictable output with minimal ongoing effort.

In the context of passive income, these capabilities translate into practical, low-friction opportunities. You might use AI to draft product descriptions, create a batch of ready-to-sell digital assets, or generate content ideas that fuel a monetized site. You might set up an email sequence that nurtures interested readers into buyers, or you might create a set of templates that you can sell again and again. The key point is that AI shifts the heavy lifting from "one-off task execution" to "reusable systems." It doesn't delete effort or risk; it changes where that effort sits and how often you need to reapply it.

Many people fear that AI will replace their jobs. The truth for most readers of this book is more nuanced: AI lowers the barrier to entry for creating value online, but it also requires a new kind of work. Instead of doing tasks manually, you design and oversee systems. You craft prompts, tune outputs, validate results, and monitor performance. You become less of a task executor and more of a system architect who ensures everything runs smoothly. That mindset—the ability to design, implement, and improve scalable processes—is the core skill that makes AI-powered income possible without endless hustling.

To keep this grounded, here are a few down-to-earth implications. AI can help you generate content ideas quickly and produce drafts you then refine. It can summarize long research into actionable notes. It can analyze data to spot trends or to optimize a marketing message for the right audience. It can also automate repetitive routines such as posting schedule management, basic customer support responses, or updating a knowledge base as you publish new information. The big win is not that you replace your brain with a machine, but that you multiply your capacity to create value with tools that work while you rest, sleep, or focus on higher-leverage tasks.

As you read, picture where AI can slide into your own work today. What task do you repeatedly do that feels ripe for automation? What content could be repurposed into multiple formats with minimal tweaks? Where can an AI-driven draft save you hours while still leaving room for your unique voice and expertise? The goal of this chapter is to give you a practical, jargon-free understanding of AI that you can translate into real, income-producing actions without needing to become a programmer or a data scientist.

THE THREE LAYERS: TOOLS, WORKFLOWS, AND SYSTEMS

Think of building an AI-powered income stream as stacking three layers that work together like a simple machine. The bottom layer is Tools. These are the apps and services you interact with directly. They are the bricks you pick up and lay down. There are many kinds of tools tailored to different tasks: content generators that draft articles, image editors that create visuals, data tools that extract insights, scheduling apps that time your posts, and translation or editing assistants that polish your writing. The important thing for beginners is to choose a focused set of tools that feel approachable. You don't need every new app; you need the right ones for the job you want to do.

The middle layer is Workflows. A workflow is the concrete sequence of steps you follow to complete a task from start to finish. It is where you connect tools so that outputs from one tool become inputs for another. A simple example might be turning an idea into a blog post. Start with a topic idea generated by AI, then have the AI draft an outline, followed by a full draft, then an editor-like pass to tighten the language, then formatting for publishing, and finally a scheduled distribution plan that pushes the post to social media and an email subscriber list. The workflow is where the magic happens because it turns a toolbox full of capabilities into a repeatable process.

The top layer is Systems. A system is the income-generating machine that runs with minimal ongoing input. It's the complete package: a workflow, the data it relies on, the audience it serves, and the monetization mechanism that pays out. A system could be a blog that continuously publishes AI-assisted content, is optimized for search and social sharing, and monetizes through affiliate links and digital product sales. It could be a service that is productized, with AI doing the heavy lifting for routine deliverables while you oversee client relations and customization. A system is not a single tool or a single task; it's the integrated arrangement of tools, workflows, and governance that yields predictable revenue over time.

Understanding this trio helps you move from chasing tools to building repeatable methods. Start by selecting a few tools that align with your goals and your comfort level. Then design a workflow that moves a raw input into a valuable output with minimal friction. Finally, assemble a system by adding a monetization mechanism, a cadence for maintenance, and a feedback loop that lets you improve the entire chain over time. In practice, you'll often be iterating through all three layers as you learn what resonates with your audience and what scales reliably.

A practical way to approach this is to begin with one simple tool you already like and a single workflow you can test in one week. As you gain confidence, you can add a second tool, expand the workflow to cover more steps, and eventually weave the whole thing into a small, self-sustaining system. You'll find that the most valuable AI projects aren't those with the most features, but those that tightly align the available tools, the sequence of actions, and a monetization path that makes sense for your time, skills, and goals.

COMMON ONLINE INCOME MODELS (PROS, CONS, AND FIT)

There is no shortage of ways to turn AI capabilities into income, but the path that works for you should fit how you want to live and what you're willing to invest. Let's walk through several popular models and talk about who they are best suited for, what to watch out for, and how AI helps them stay scalable. One approach is to start with digital products. These are assets you create once and sell again and again. AI can help in two powerful ways: it can generate the content and design templates that form the product, and it can update and customize those assets over time so they stay fresh. Think of digital planners, checklists, editable templates, or short guides that solve a clear problem. The upside is obvious: you make a single piece of work and keep earning from it. The downside is the upfront time to craft something compelling and the ongoing need to refresh or expand the catalog to maintain relevance.

Another route is affiliate marketing and niche sites. You build a site or a newsletter that recommends products and earns commissions when readers buy through your links. AI shines here by helping you discover profitable niches, generate high-quality content, and optimize how you present offers. The catch is that traffic and trust matter as much as the content itself. You'll need to learn a bit about audience needs, search intent, and credible recommendations, because a well-targeted audience can yield steady commissions and a more forgiving churn rate when you stay helpful rather than overly promotional.

A third option is services, especially productized or semi-automated services. You can define concrete deliverables, set standard pricing, and use AI to scale the routine parts of the work—think resume polishing, website copy packages, or market research briefs. The beauty of this path is you can start with what you know and gradually automate the repetitive pieces. The risk is that you still have some client interaction and quality control to maintain. The best practice is to build a framework where client expectations are clearly defined, and your system reliably delivers the core value with minimal custom tweaking each time.

Niche sites, membership areas, or micro-SaaS ideas are other common routes people explore. AI can help with keyword research, content generation, product updates, and dashboards that track performance. The big trade-offs here are the time you'll need to invest in building traffic and the patience required to see results. None of these models is a guaranteed, overnight windfall, but each becomes powerful when you blend a solid audience understanding with repeatable processes and a clear path to monetization.

To make this more concrete, imagine a small beginner who wants to get started quickly without feeling overwhelmed. They might choose a digital product in a niche they know well and couple it with one simple affiliate offer. If time allows, they could layer in an automations-backed newsletter that promotes the product and a few related tools. Or they might start a micro-site focused on a narrow topic with AI helping generate weekly content and update product recommendations as new options appear. The key is to pick one or two paths that feel doable and align with your skills, then test them for a few weeks to gauge traction. As you experiment, you'll begin to see patterns—what audiences respond to, which monetization hooks work, and how much maintenance is truly needed to keep the machine humming."

ACTIVE VS. PASSIVE VS. SET AND MAINTAIN

When people hear the word passive, they often imagine a system that requires no attention at all. In reality, the best AI-driven income streams require regular, purposeful maintenance. Active income is the portion of the work you do yourself—creating new content, reaching out to potential partners, or tweaking offers in response to feedback. Passive income is the dream—income that keeps flowing with little day-to-day effort—but in practice it is usually supported by systems that you maintain on a set schedule. And then there is the middle ground, which you could call "set and maintain": a machine that runs but still needs periodic tuning, updates, and quality checks to stay reliable.

A healthy way to think about this is to separate the initial build from ongoing upkeep. The upfront phase is where you devote time to design the system: choosing tools, wiring the workflow together, and summoning the motivation to ship something that people can actually use. Once the system is in motion, the ongoing work usually shifts toward monitoring performance, updating content as needed, refreshing offers, and handling edge cases that come up in real life. The key point is that maintenance isn't a dirty word; it's part of any sustainable income stream. A dashboard showing traffic, revenue, and conversion rates becomes your daily task list, and your goal is to keep those numbers moving in a favorable direction.

Misleading headlines aside, very few truly passive income streams exist in a vacuum. Even the simplest digital product needs occasional updates for new platforms, changing trends, or evolving consumer needs. An affiliate site benefits from regular content refreshes and periodic SEO tweaks. A productized service works best when you automate the routine but still perform periodic quality checks and client communications. The moment you forget to check, a small misalignment can cascade into lost sales or deteriorating trust. Therefore, frame your expectations around a core principle: set up a system that you can monitor efficiently, and dedicate time to optimizing rather than endlessly adding more features.

With this mindset, you'll avoid the common pitfall of over-engineering the dream of "set and forget." You'll instead aim for a lean, reliable machine that provides steady value with a predictable cadence. That approach makes it much easier to scale, because you know what works, what to tweak, and how to replicate the success in other domains without reinventing the wheel each time.

CHOOSING THE RIGHT PATH BASED ON TIME, MONEY, AND SKILLS

Choosing a path is less about chasing the hottest trend and more about aligning your resources with a clear, testable plan. Start by taking a calm inventory of three things: time you can commit each week, money you're willing to invest upfront, and the skills you already have or are excited to learn. A realistic self-assessment is your compass: it prevents you from chasing models that require dozens of hours of coding or a substantial budget you don't have.

If you have only a few hours a week and little seed money, the gentlest, fastest route is to start with a small, one-tool workflow that solves a real problem and can be monetized through a simple model like digital products or a light affiliate setup. With a bit more time, you can layer in another tool to automate a second step and gradually assemble a two-tool workflow, then a tiny system that earns a modest recurring revenue. If your starting point includes even a modest budget and you enjoy curating ideas, a niche site with AI-assisted content and affiliate monetization can be a compelling long-term project. If you have professional skills you can package, productized services offer a clear route: you scale your impact by letting AI handle the mundane parts while you focus on client value and relationship building.

As you test ideas, look for signals that a model is working: a handful of customers, consistent traffic, or repeat buyers. Your aim is not a perfect first hit but a learn-or-die loop that confirms what your audience values and how much you can automate without losing trust. It's perfectly acceptable to start with one model and then add another once you've proven the core system. A quiet, disciplined approach beats a loud, scattershot one. You'll also want to consider risk tolerance, legal considerations, and the ethical dimension of your chosen approach. The most durable paths are those that respect your audience, deliver real value, and can be maintained over time without burning you out.

If you're unsure where to begin, a practical tactic is to pick two starter models that feel accessible—perhaps one digital product and one affiliate approach—and set a four-to-six-week window to validate them. During that window, you'll design a single workflow for each model, build the minimum viable system, and measure key indicators like sign-ups, downloads, clicks, or revenue. If the numbers don't move in the direction you hoped, either pivot to a different approach within the same framework or scale back to a simpler variant that you can execute more confidently. The important part is to start with something you can ship quickly, learn from honestly, and iterate toward something you can sustain.

The more you practice choosing paths with a practical lens, the better you'll become at spotting the opportunities that fit your life. You'll start to see the patterns behind successful combinations of tools, workflows, and monetization strategies, and you'll begin to assemble a small portfolio of income streams that are resilient, diversified, and scalable.

THE MINDSET SHIFT: FROM DOING TASKS TO DESIGNING SYSTEMS

The most transformative idea in this book is not a new AI trick, but a shift in how you think about work. If you're used to trading time for money—doing tasks, delivering deliverables, and chasing busywork—AI has the potential to free you from that pattern. The real power lies in adopting a design mindset: you are not merely performing tasks; you are sketching and tuning a system that creates value with minimal ongoing effort.

Designing systems demands a clear mental map. You start with a goal—such as "generate steady income from a content machine" or "deliver a productized service with reliable delivery" —and you work backward from that goal to identify the ingredients: the tools you'll use, the steps that will automate those steps, and the monetization mechanism that makes it financially meaningful. Along the way you establish guardrails: the guidelines that ensure the outputs stay useful and ethical, the checks that keep quality consistent, and the boundaries that protect your time and energy.

Metrics become your compass. You track revenue, traffic, engagement, and the rate at which you can push updates or improvements through the system. You define a maintenance rhythm—when to refresh content, how often to audit links, when to update offers—and you schedule it so it doesn't disrupt your life. Documentation becomes a core habit: every workflow, tool configuration, and decision rule is written down so you or someone else can pick up where you left off. This is not about rigid compliance; it's about predictable outcomes and the freedom that comes with knowing exactly how your machine works.

Ethics and sustainability deserve a prominent place in your planning. The best AI systems respect your audience's trust, avoid manipulation, and strive for transparent disclosure about AI involvement. You should be mindful of changing platform policies and legal requirements around data, advertising, and content ownership. The most durable income streams are those built on genuine value, not on shortcuts that break trust or rely on exploiting loopholes. As you adopt this mindset, you'll find yourself asking better questions: How can I automate more of this without sacrificing quality? What range of tasks can AI handle so I can focus on strategy and relationships? How can I keep learning and adapting as technology and markets evolve?

In the end, the shift from doing tasks to designing systems is a shift toward leverage. With a well-designed system, your time multiplies. Your income scales beyond what you could accomplish alone, and your work becomes more sustainable because you are building something that can endure changes in tools, platforms, or trends. This is the core promise of AI-powered passive income: not a shortcut, but a smarter, longer-term way to create value for others—and for you.

TWO
OPPORTUNITY DISCOVERY – FINDING PROFITABLE PROBLEMS AI CAN HELP SOLVE

START WITH PROBLEMS, NOT TOOLS: WHY COOL TECH ISN'T ENOUGH

When people first stumble into AI for income, they often chase the latest feature or the flashiest tool. They look at dashboards full of numbers and wonder which widget will unlock their next payday. The real truth, though, is simpler and more stubborn: customers don't pay for novelty. They pay for relief from a pain they actually feel. And if your product or service doesn't address a pain point with clarity and speed, more features won't fix that gap.

This idea may feel obvious, but it's astonishing how easy it is to drift toward the "cool tech" mindset. AI can generate content, forecast trends, and automate repetitive tasks. That's impressive. But potential buyers don't care about your clever algorithm until they see that it saves them time, money, or stress. A tool that sounds amazing in a pitch deck can fall flat in the wild if the problem you're solving is vague or optional.

The practical flip side is empowering. If you anchor your idea in a real problem, you can sketch a solution that's plausible to a nontechnical audience. Start with a vivid description of the pain. How long does it take to complete the task today? How often does the work slip or require rework? How much money or opportunity does the delay cost? When you can describe the pain with some quantitative touchpoints—minutes wasted per day, dollars spent on a suboptimal process, the cognitive load of managing messy data—you've created a bridge to a real offer.

A reliable path to profitable problems begins with empathy and curiosity. Listen to the people who will buy your solution as if you were conducting a customer interview, but do it without jargon. You'll hear phrases like "I wish there was a simple way to keep track of X," or "I hate how long it takes me to Y," or "This report always comes out wrong and I have to redo it." Those are not just complaints; they're signals. They point to a faster route to value. If you can translate those signals into a promise— save me time, save me money, or reduce my stress—you're almost there.

In practice, you'll want to develop a simple, repeatable lens for evaluation: does this pain repeat across many people? is it costly enough to justify a solution? can a reproducible process powered by AI drastically reduce the burden? If the answer to these questions is yes, you've found ammunition for a real opportunity. If the pain is rare, unique to one person, or too vague to measure, it's a sign to reframe or pivot.

The point is not to pick the first pain you hear but to validate that a genuine, scalable cost of inaction exists. A scalable cost means many people would benefit in roughly the same way, and a viable solution would scale without becoming a swamp of bespoke customization. In the end, the most sustainable AI-driven income streams come from problems that people are actively trying to solve and will pay to solve quickly and consistently.

WHERE TO LOOK: FORUMS, REVIEWS, SOCIAL MEDIA, AND YOUR OWN WORK

Opportunity rarely announces itself with a neon sign. It shows up in the quiet corners of forums, in stubborn customer reviews, and in the small annoyances you encounter in your own daily workflow. The best ideas emerge when you collect whispers from multiple sources and notice converging patterns. You don't need a PhD in data science to read the room; you need a willingness to listen where people already talk about their problems.

Forums are fertile ground because people use them to vent, compare, and seek help. Reddit threads, specialized communities, and even product-specific boards echo what frustrates people in real life. Look for recurring complaints: users wishing for faster results, fewer steps, more accurate outputs, or easier onboarding. You'll also notice where users praise certain features or lament missing ones. Those gaps are prime targets for AI-enabled solutions that can deliver at scale.

Reviews are another goldmine. People are honest when they're told a product or service will be improved in a forthcoming update or when it falls short. Read dozens of reviews across products that are tangential to your idea. You'll often uncover a thread of requests—whether it's better data organization, more reliable automation, or clearer instructions—that reveals a universal ache. Don't dismiss seemingly minor complaints; a small annoyance, amplified across thousands of users, compounds into a meaningful opportunity.

Social media adds a different flavor. Short posts, live streams, and comments reveal current sentiment and trending complaints. A user might gripe about "too many tabs," "manual data entry," or "export formats that never align." These surface signals are powerful when they point in the same direction across platforms. The beauty of social media is velocity: you can spot nascent problems before they become mainstream issues, allowing you to be early to the solution.

Your own work is a secret weapon. If you're a freelancer, employee, or small business owner, you know the tasks you endure day after day. The pain you tolerate is likely shared by someone else. Start by journaling your week for two to three days. Note every task that feels repetitive, frustrating, or error-prone. Watch for moments when you think, "There has to be an easier way." Those are targets for AI automation. If you run a small operation, audit your standard operating procedures. Where do you slip on accuracy, where do you waste time coordinating between tools, and where do customers complain about delays? Your own workflow holds a blueprint of the market's unmet needs.

To turn these sources into a concrete opportunity, you need a disciplined filter. The filter is simple: does this pain align with at least three sources or three different people? Is it something a scalable process could fix with a repeatable workflow? And is the problem solvable with a practical amount of AI assistance given current tools? If you can answer yes to these questions, you've identified a doable opportunity worth exploring further. If you can't, you haven't failed; you've saved yourself time from chasing a mirage. The point is to build a pipeline of ideas rooted in real conversations and real needs, not clever tech fantasies.

PATTERNS OF PROFITABLE PROBLEMS (SAVE TIME, SAVE MONEY, REDUCE STRESS)

Profitable problems tend to fall into recognizable patterns. They repeat themselves across people, industries, and price ranges. When you map pains to patterns, you create a sturdy framework for choosing opportunities that scale with AI. There are three core patterns that consistently translate into paid solutions: Save Time, Save Money, and Reduce Stress. Each pattern has its own flavor and sweet spots, but they also overlap, which is where the best opportunities live.

Save Time is about cutting the clock from task to result. Time is the most fungible resource in most people's lives. If a process takes hours, days, or repeated cycles that don't end, there's room for automation. AI shines here by automating repetitive reasoning, curating information, and performing tasks with high consistency. Imagine an assistant that can read dozens of documents, extract the key facts, and draft a summary in minutes. Or a workflow that automatically organizes incoming emails, schedules meetings, and surfaces the right data to you with almost no manual input. The people who benefit most are those who juggle multiple responsibilities and feel the pinch of every minute wasted. The payoff isn't flashy; it's predictable and tangible, which makes it a reliable basis for an income stream that can run in the background.

Save Money targets the friction points that drain budgets. Costs accumulate through waste, misalignment, and errors. AI can reduce those costs by improving accuracy, consolidating steps, and optimizing choices. Think of a business owner who spends on outsourced reporting that's inconsistent or a freelancer who loses hours to manual data entry. An AI-powered system that pre-fills reports, reconciles invoices, or negotiates price comparisons can save real dollars over time. What makes this pattern attractive is the direct line from capability to cash, especially in areas like bookkeeping, procurement, or customer care where tiny improvements scale into big savings.

Reduce Stress addresses the cognitive load and emotional burden of decision making. When a process demands high attention, presents conflicting data, or requires rapid judgment, stress climbs. AI can become a calmer, steadier partner, offering consistent recommendations, clean dashboards, and timely reminders. A tool that helps a busy creator decide which idea to pursue next, or a system that surfaces the most likely customer questions before a live chat, lowers mental friction and makes outcomes more reliable. The financial signal here is risk reduction: fewer mistakes, fewer misses, and fewer burnout days that translate into better retention and longer-term income.

These patterns aren't box checkers; they're lenses. When you evaluate a potential problem, scan for which pattern it primarily triggers and whether AI can meaningfully accelerate the outcome. The strongest opportunities often deliver a blend: save time while cutting costs, or save time and reduce stress, with a measurable uplift in consistency and quality. The beauty of this approach is that it keeps you anchored to real value while giving you a clear route to a repeatable, scalable solution rather than a one-off magic trick.

USING AI TO SPEED UP MARKET RESEARCH

Market research feels intimidating to non-technical readers, but with AI it becomes a practical, repeatable habit rather than a distant chore. The core idea is simple: use AI to process large amounts of information quickly so you can see patterns you would have missed by reading a handful of sources. This isn't about replacing human judgment; it's about speeding up the discovery phase so you can move from "could this be a thing?" to "this is likely a thing" faster and with more confidence.

Begin with a clearly defined research question. What problem are you trying to validate? What would a successful outcome look like in measurable terms—time saved, money saved, or a quantifiable reduction in error? With that anchor, you gather diverse inputs: long-form articles, product reviews, forum threads, influencer discussions, and even your own recent work tasks. AI shines in taking that mass of text and turning it into something digestible: key themes, recurrent phrases, and top pain points. Instead of sifting through hundreds of pages, you get a concise map of the landscape and a prioritization of the most urgent problems.

One practical workflow is to collect a broad set of sources that touch your target audience. Run each source through a summarization pass to extract main ideas and pain points. Then run a clustering pass to group similar issues together. The result is a library of pain statements, each tagged with frequency and implied impact. The next step is synthesis: draft problem statements that feel concrete and actionable, each accompanied by a rough picture of what a viable AI solution could look like and what the first test would involve. You'll often discover that a surprising number of sources converge on the same issue or in different words describe a common obstacle. That convergence is a green flag that you're looking at a real opportunity.

Prompts don't have to be fancy to be effective. You can guide the AI with prompts like: summarize the top three recurring complaints in this collection, extract the most common phrases that signal a time bottleneck, or group these concerns into save time, save money, and reduce stress categories. You're not chasing perfect data; you're looking for directional signals strong enough to justify a low-risk validation. The aim is to turn a sea of qualitative information into a focused set of problem statements that are easy to test with a simple, low-cost experiment.

As you become more comfortable, you'll learn to layer in quick competitive checks. What are the closest alternatives doing well, and where are they failing the user? Where do gaps exist between what people say they want and what current products actually deliver? The value of AI here isn't precision alone; it's speed, scope, and the confidence to move forward without waiting for a perfect, perfect dataset. In short, AI accelerates the discovery cycle so you can reach a practical, testable hypothesis sooner rather than later.

SIMPLE VALIDATION: SURVEYS, PRE-SALES, AND SMALL TESTS

Validation is the quiet anchor that saves you from building something that nobody wants. It doesn't require you to quit your job and bet everything on a single product; it asks only for small, low-risk bets that reveal interest or willingness to pay. The simplest form is a quick survey, but in practical terms a validation plan is a story you tell the market that you're testing a specific promise: if we build this, you'll get this outcome, and you're willing to pay for it. The trick is to design validation so it's easy for people to respond honestly without feeling manipulated or misled.

A short survey can be as simple as a handful of questions that measure interest and price tolerance. You want to capture two things: whether the pain is real and whether your proposed fix feels worth paying for. Phrase questions around outcomes rather than features. Instead of asking, "Would you like an AI tool that does X?" ask, "If this tool could save you 3 hours a week, would you pay $X for it?" The goal is to surface a credible signal—positive or negative—without spinning a yarn that invites false positives.

Pre-sales are the next step up. A landing page with a clear promise and a minimal signup can gauge demand before you build the full product. Offer early access, a waitlist, or a pilot program with a nominal fee or a refundable deposit. The key is to create a tangible commitment signal. When people say yes in enough numbers, you have real validation that the problem exists and that there is a willingness to invest now, not later in a hypothetical future.

Small tests are your experiments in the wild. Build the smallest viable version of your idea and push it to a restricted audience. It could be a freemium version that demonstrates the core automation, or a single workflow that handles one repeatable task for a set of customers. Then measure what happens next: how many people engage, how often they use the feature, whether the promised outcome happens, and whether they are willing to pay—or upgrade—to a more capable version. The insights from these tests are gold because they come from real user behavior, not from hypothetical scenarios.

Ethics and honesty matter in validation. Be transparent about what you're testing, what the user gets, and what data you're collecting. Misleading people—even unintentionally—can damage your reputation and undermine future opportunities. The right approach is to communicate clearly, offer a real value proposition, and be prepared to adjust or pivot if the market's response is cooler than you expected. Validation is not a gate to doom; it's a shield that protects your time, your budget, and your credibility.

CHOOSING YOUR FIRST AI INCOME IDEA: NARROWING FROM MANY OPTIONS TO ONE

You've spent time listening, mapping patterns, and testing assumptions. Now comes the delicate moment: choosing one AI income idea to start with. The best starting idea is not the one with the most brilliant feature, but the one with a clean path to value, a reasonable learning curve, and a clear route to market. A practical way to decide is to evaluate ideas along three dimensions: difficulty or learning curve, potential upside or revenue ceiling, and personal alignment with your skills and interests. This triad helps you avoid chasing ideas that sound exciting but would take years to monetize or would require skills you don't want to master.

Begin by listing your top three candidates. For each idea, sketch a rough map: what is the core outcome for the customer, what is the minimal AI support required to deliver that outcome, and what would be the first trigger step a customer takes to engage with you. Then ask a simple set of questions: How long will it take me to reach the first milestone? What is the lowest device footprint and operational cost I can start with? What is the simplest price point and delivery model that could work— subscription, one-time purchase, or a service add-on? By making it practical, you avoid paralysis borne of endless possibilities.

A helpful heuristic is to rank ideas by the speed to market. A speed to value mindset often wins because it gives you a real user signal quickly. If you can launch a tiny, credible version within a few weeks and prove the concept with real customers, you gain a powerful advantage. Another useful lens is to estimate your personal learning value. If the best idea forces you to learn a lot of new skills, you may be building a durable capability that compounds over time, but you'll also need more time and energy. If the upside is strong but you can't sustain the learning pace, you may want to pause and choose a softer path first.

Freedom from burnout and the desire for a sustainable pace should factor into your choice. The ideal first project is one that you can run with minimal day-to-day friction, yet provides a reliable signal of customer interest. It should be automatable enough that the ongoing effort remains predictable, even if you're not actively tinkering. The moment you decide on one idea, turn your focus there and commit to a small, concrete plan—no more vacillation. Remember, this isn't the finish line; it's your first stepping stone toward a scalable AI-powered income that can compound over time.

THREE

YOUR AI TOOLBELT – ESSENTIAL TOOLS FOR NON-TECHNICAL BEGINNERS

CORE CATEGORIES: WHERE AI MEETS YOUR INCOME STREAMS

Imagine your income engine built from five dependable tool families, each doing a distinct job but designed to work in harmony. This is the core idea behind your AI toolbelt. The five categories—Text, Images, Video, Audio, and Automation—cover the main kinds of work you'll automate or augment with AI. Text tools help you generate content, craft persuasive messages, draft emails, and respond to customers with speed and consistency. Images tools let you create visuals, thumbnails, banners, and social assets that grab attention without hiring a designer for every post. Video tools enable you to build short, shareable clips and simple moving assets that enrich your marketing without requiring expensive editing software. Audio tools let you produce podcasts, voiceovers, or narrated explainers that scale beyond your own speaking hours. Automation platforms act as the glue, moving data between tools, triggering workflows, and keeping your system humming without manual clicks. The beauty of this toolkit is in the combinations. A single blog post can become a long-form article, a set of social posts, an email in your sequence, a thumbnail, a short video, and an audio version—all generated with a handful of reliable tools and a well-designed workflow.

When you start with these five families, you're not building a single asset. You're building a repeatable process. You're creating a small, scalable machine that can produce content, drive traffic, nurture leads, and close sales while you focus on new ideas or simply enjoy your time. The goal is not to chase every new app but to assemble a stable stack of tools that you understand deeply and can maintain over time. In practice, you'll want to pick one credible option per category and use them to support a single income stream or a few related streams. As you grow, you can extend your belt by layering in additional tools that complement your core choices. The key is consistency, not complexity. If your workflow feels heavy or brittle, you'll burn out or miss opportunities. If it feels light, obvious, and reliable, you'll keep momentum and see results.

This section lays the groundwork for practical, beginner-friendly workflows. You'll learn how each category contributes to a passive income model and how to assemble simple pipelines that run with minimal ongoing effort. Think of Text as your content engine, Images as your visual amplifier, Video and Audio as your reach multipliers, and Automation as your steady hand guiding every piece of the system. The good news is that you don't need to be a coder to wield these tools effectively. You need a plan, a few dependable applications, and a clear picture of how the pieces fit together. You'll get that plan here, with concrete examples, prompts you can adapt, and a straightforward path from idea to execution.

As you begin selecting tools, remember this: cheaper, simpler options that you actually use are worth more than grand ambitions with no follow-through. Your instruction to your toolkit is not to maximize fancy features but to enable reliable, long-term performance. With the right combination, you'll build an asset that doesn't demand your full attention every day but still pays you back over time. That's the essence of a practical AI toolbelt for non-technical beginners who want real, sustainable passive income.

AI FOR TEXT: WORDS THAT WORK FOR YOU

Text is the backbone of most online income systems. It's where your audience discovers you, learns from you, and decides to trust you enough to buy or engage. With AI, your words can carry more weight, arrive faster, and be more consistent than ever before. The approach is not to replace human judgment but to amplify it—creating a high-quality draft that you can refine rather than starting from scratch every time. A typical workflow begins with a clear sense of audience and purpose. You identify the outcome you want from the text—an article, a sales page, an email sequence, or a customer reply—and you craft a precise prompt that sets the tone, outlines the structure, and provides any key data points you want included. From there the AI does the heavy lifting: it produces an outline, expands into a full draft, and offers variations to test in different channels. The real skill lies in shaping prompts, guiding the tone, and editing the output so it truly fits your voice and your value proposition.

A practical example might look like this in practice. You have a niche topic and a basic audience persona. You prompt the AI to draft a 1200-word blog post with a friendly, practical voice and a headline that promises a concrete benefit. The draft comes back with sections, a logical flow, and callouts for examples. You then refine the opening, add a personal anecdote, and inject a few data points or citations. The AI can produce a version tailored for SEO, embedding keywords naturally without turning the piece into keyword stuffing. After that, you generate a punchy email sequence to promote the post, pulling key quotes and a short summary for each email. You can also create short social posts derived from the article's highlights, preserving your voice and framing.

The beauty of AI text for passive income is its adaptability. You might use it to draft evergreen product guides, write outreach emails that land in a prospect's inbox with a gentle, human touch, or reply to customer inquiries with consistent messaging. To stay sustainable, establish templates you reuse across projects. Save your best prompts, save your signature phrases, and curate a small bank of high-performing subject lines and intros. Over time, your prompts become your most valuable asset, because they shape outputs that consistently move readers toward action. Remember to review for accuracy, tone, and compliance with your brand—AI shines in speed and breadth, but your judgment still sets the standard for quality and trust. And when you're testing ideas, use a subset of your audience or an internal test list to minimize risk, then scale what works.

For beginners, the aim is to reach a comfortable balance between automation and touch. Let AI draft and edit, but retain the final pass for alignment with your brand and your ethics. This is where your business grows—not by chasing perfection in every sentence but by delivering reliable, useful content that your audience values and that supports predictable revenue over time.

AI FOR MEDIA: VISUALS THAT SCALE YOUR REACH

In the real world, people judge quickly by what they see. Great visuals capture attention, establish credibility, and explain complex ideas in seconds. AI for media helps you generate and refine images, thumbnails, banners, and short videos that look professional without hiring a designer or spending hours fiddling with layers. The goal is to create a cohesive visual language you can repeat across your blog, homepage, social channels, and product pages. Start with a simple visual system: a consistent color palette, a few typography choices, and a handful of templates for different formats. AI can generate images from prompts, enhance existing photos, or remix stock visuals into something uniquely yours. When used responsibly, AI-generated visuals can be a powerful multiplier for your income streams.

Consider a project where you launch a new digital guide. You begin with a hero image that conveys the guide's core benefit. You then craft a set of social thumbnails—one main design and a few variations to test across platforms. The AI helps you iterate quickly: it can adjust color contrasts for readability, refine composition for mobile screens, and generate variations that line up with your brand's look. The same approach applies to short videos. You can assemble a simple storyboard, produce a few captioned clips, and export versions tailored for Instagram, YouTube Shorts, and TikTok. AI-assisted video captions and auto-transcription make your content accessible, which broadens your audience and improves engagement.

Brand safety matters just as much in visuals as in text. Use your templates and presets to maintain a recognizable voice and appearance. If you're using stock imagery or AI-generated visuals, keep a log of licensing terms and ensure you're compliant with platform policies. Also be mindful of ethical considerations—avoid deepfakes or misleading representations, and clearly label AI-assisted visuals where appropriate. In practice, a small, repeatable visual system saves you time while preserving quality. You'll be able to publish more frequently, experiment with different formats, and scale your content without sacrificing consistency or credibility. That's the power of AI-enabled media for passive income: you create assets once and reuse them across channels to reach more people with less effort.

NO-CODE AUTOMATION PLATFORMS: THE GLUE THAT BINDS YOUR TOOLS

Automation platforms are the invisible engine room of your business. They connect your text, media, and publishing tools in a seamless workflow so a single action

—like publishing a blog post—sets off a chain of helpful tasks. No-code automation is not about replacing human work; it's about orchestrating activities so you can step back and let the system do the repetitive parts. The core idea is simple: triggers, actions, and data. A trigger starts the workflow when a defined event happens. An action performs a task, and data flows from one tool to another with minimal manual input. The strength of these platforms lies in their accessibility. You can build and adjust automations with a visual interface, dragging and dropping blocks that represent steps in your process. To keep things manageable, start with one or two core automations that directly support revenue. For example, when you publish a new article, the automation could generate social media posts, queue a thumbnail design, and deliver an email notification to your list. As you grow, you layer in additional steps: add a follow-up email, post snippets to a community forum, create a task in your project board, or update your content calendar.

The right automation approach makes your income streams feel almost effortless. You don't need complex software to run a six-figure dream; you need reliable, well-designed flows. A practical note for beginners: choose automation tools with friendly price points, clear documentation, and secure data handling. Keep an eye on execution times and failure rates. A workflow that occasionally stalls becomes a friction point for your audience and your own motivation. Build your automations with clear ownership and test them in a low-risk environment before you wire them into your live site or storefront. Documentation matters. Write short notes about what each automation does, what data it uses, and what outcomes you expect. This isn't just about saving time; it's about preserving control so you can adjust, improve, or scale your system as your audience and revenue grow.

As you become more confident, you'll see patterns emerge: content dissemination, lead capture and nurturing, customer support routing, and sales process automation. You'll learn to leverage the automation platform as a backbone, while your AI tools handle the creative work. The result is a lean, responsive system that operates with minimal day-to-day oversight. You'll have a reliable spine for your income machine, one that can adapt to new ideas without collapsing under the weight of complexity.

ORGANIZING YOUR STACK: SIMPLE, CHEAP, AND MAINTAINABLE

If you chase every shiny tool, you'll end up with a cluttered toolbox and a confusing workflow. The smartest approach for non-technical beginners is to start small with a clearly defined, budget-conscious stack and a plan for maintenance. Your goal is a minimal but capable toolkit that you can actually manage over weeks and months, not days. A practical starter stack focuses on five core areas: a text tool for content and messaging, a media tool for visuals, a video or audio utility for short-form media, a no-code automation platform to tie everything together, and a storage or workflow hub to keep assets organized. Within each category, you pick one trusted option and learn it deeply. This reduces friction, speeds up execution, and helps you build muscle memory around prompts, file naming, and version control.

Give yourself boundaries that keep costs predictable. Start with free tiers or low-cost plans you can sustain even if revenue is modest. As your income grows or your needs become more demanding, you can upgrade thoughtfully. The idea is to avoid vendor lock-in by choosing tools that offer straightforward data export and a reasonable path to migration. And always design for long-term maintenance. Create simple naming conventions for files and prompts; document your standard prompts and templates; keep a single hub for your assets, like a cloud folder with a predictable structure; and maintain a short, human-friendly changelog of automation updates. A lean stack also means you're mindful of data flow. Map where data originates, where it travels, and where it ends up. This clarity reduces the risk of data leaks, misuses, or compliance problems, and it makes onboarding someone else easier if you ever bring in help or a partner.

Finally, remember that tools exist to serve you, not the other way around. If a tool slows you down, it's time to reassess. If a feature you're paying for isn't adding measurable value, cut it. The smartest builders stay lean because they know that simplicity compounds over time. Your aim is a practical, budget-savvy stack that you can traverse confidently. When you look at your toolkit, you should feel ready to launch, not overwhelmed by choices. The right setup is the one you actually use consistently— the one that turns your ideas into repeatable revenue without draining your time or your will to build.

SAFETY AND PRIVACY BASICS WHEN USING AI TOOLS

Ethical use and prudent risk management aren't afterthoughts; they're the foundation of a sustainable income built with AI. As you assemble your toolbelt, you'll encounter questions about data, privacy, and trust. The first rule is simple: don't upload anything you wouldn't want to be public or permanently archived. This includes sensitive client information, personal data, or confidential business documents. Treat customer data with care, anonymize wherever possible, and keep detailed internal notes about what data is used for what purpose. The second principle is guardrails for your own business. Use strong, unique passwords for every service, enable two-factor authentication where available, and rotate API keys on a schedule or whenever you suspect a compromise.

Keep a secure record of your credentials and never paste them into chat windows or shared documents. Your automation platforms should be configured with restricted access, and you should audit who can modify workflows.

API keys are the lifeblood of AI-powered workflows, but they're also a vulnerability if mishandled. Treat keys like valuable inventory: store them in a secure vault, restrict their permissions to the minimum necessary, and revoke them if a project ends or someone leaves your team. When you're building customer-facing solutions, you'll likely face terms of service questions about data usage. Read the provider's privacy policy and terms carefully. Some platforms train their models on user content unless you opt out; others give you explicit control over data retention. If you're unsure, choose services with transparent data practices and a clear opt-out path. You also want to design for safety in outputs. Always review AI-generated text and media for accuracy, avoid harmful or misleading content, and be transparent with your audience about what is AI-generated when appropriate. It's not just about legality; it's about preserving your credibility and your readers' trust.

Finally, design your workflows with resilience in mind. Build in defaults that catch errors, such as not publishing to a live site without human review, or sending test emails to a private list before you reach customers. Treat your first few projects as learning experiments, not as final products. This mindset helps you spot blind spots early—like outputs that deviate from your brand voice or images that don't align with your audience's sensibilities. Over time, you'll develop a mature, ethical, and safe approach to AI that protects you and your audience while still delivering the efficiency and scale that passive income demands.

FOUR
DESIGNING AUTOMATED CONTENT MACHINES

THE CONTENT ENGINE: INPUTS, PROCESS, OUTPUTS

Think of content creation as a small factory that never sleeps. A well-designed content engine takes raw inputs, runs them through a repeatable workflow, and outputs publish-ready material on a reliable schedule. The power of this approach lies not in one brilliant stroke but in a living system you can reproduce again and again, with the results improving as you learn what works and what doesn't. In practice, you assemble three core elements: inputs, the process, and outputs. When you picture these elements as a single pipeline, the path from idea to published post becomes predictable rather than mysterious, scalable rather than heroic, and ultimately capable of supporting a growing stream of passive income.

Inputs are everything you bring into the system. They include your audience profile—who you're writing for, what keeps them up at night, and what kind of promise they're seeking. They also include topic themes you've identified as valuable, keywords and search intent you've researched, your brand voice and stance, and any source materials you rely on for accuracy. You may also collect data from your own past content, engagement metrics, and feedback from readers or viewers. The more structured your inputs, the more consistent your outputs will be. This is where your content strategy begins to take shape: a clear sense of who you serve, what you produce, and how you'll say it.

The process is the engine room. It is the set of steps that converts inputs into tangible content. This typically starts with prompts or templates that tell the AI what to produce, followed by an editing loop where you shape the draft to fit your voice and standards. In a mature system, the process is modular: you reuse prompts across different formats, you reuse tone and length controls, and you reuse a style guide that keeps your writing recognizable. The workflow also includes scheduling and distribution steps so the content appears on your blog, in a newsletter, or across social channels on a regular cadence. The key is to separate the decision points from the execution: decide what output you want first, then let the engine assemble the pieces. When you design prompts with consistent structure—introduction, core sections,

OSING A NICHE AND PLATFORM

sing where your content will live and what you'll
bout is the first big design decision for your content
e. The right niche isn't just about passion; it's about
ainability, audience demand, and your capacity to
ver consistently. Likewise, the platform you choose
suld align with your format strengths and the prefer-
eres of your target readers or viewers. Start by asking
three questions: what topics am I excited to explore week
after week, where do people search for answers in this
space, and what format can I sustain without burning out?

A strong niche has three traits: it solves a real problem, it's
specific enough to stand out, and it has a reasonable audience size that grows over time. If a niche is too broad,
your content can feel generic and hard to differentiate. If
it's too narrow, you risk a fragile audience that dries up
quickly. The platform you pick should play to your
strengths and the rhythm you can sustain. Blogs excel at
dth and SEO, newsletters offer direct access to a loyal
aience and high engagement, YouTube rewards consis-
, well-produced video with strong retention, and
al channels reward quick experimentation and
time conversation.

about your strengths as a creator. If you're a good
who enjoys research, a blog plus a weekly news-
an be a powerful combination. If you like speaking
rytelling, YouTube or a podcast feed supported by

examples, and a takeaway—you r\
outputs aligned with your goals.

Outputs are the public face of your engi\
articles, newsletters, social posts, vide\
podcasts that your audience will see, read,\
with. Outputs should be flexible enough to\
multiple channels. A robust content engine pi\
base piece that can be repurposed: a long ble\
becomes a shorter article, a video script, and a set of\
captions; a newsletter issue becomes a blog post ai\
series of micro-posts for social media. This is where y\
measure the system's impact. Are your posts attracting\
your target audience? Do they spark replies, shares, and\
saves? Are you building a reliable cadence that readers\
come to expect? The outputs are not a one-off spectacle\
but a library of material that compounds in value as it si\
in front of more people over time.

Building a content engine is a practical exercise in\
pline and system design. Start with a simple, rep\
workflow, then broaden the inputs and output\
learn. The aim is to reach a point where you ca\
few prompts, feed the system a short list of\
watch a predictable stream of publish-re\
emerge with minimal ongoing effort. Whe\
content this way, your passive income\
more achievable, because you've replac\
a reliable machine that serves your\
sleep.

examples, and a takeaway—you reduce drift and keep outputs aligned with your goals.

Outputs are the public face of your engine. They are the articles, newsletters, social posts, video scripts, or podcasts that your audience will see, read, and engage with. Outputs should be flexible enough to flow into multiple channels. A robust content engine produces a base piece that can be repurposed: a long blog post becomes a shorter article, a video script, and a set of social captions; a newsletter issue becomes a blog post and a series of micro-posts for social media. This is where you measure the system's impact. Are your posts attracting your target audience? Do they spark replies, shares, and saves? Are you building a reliable cadence that readers come to expect? The outputs are not a one-off spectacle but a library of material that compounds in value as it sits in front of more people over time.

Building a content engine is a practical exercise in discipline and system design. Start with a simple, repeatable workflow, then broaden the inputs and outputs as you learn. The aim is to reach a point where you can set up a few prompts, feed the system a short list of topics, and watch a predictable stream of publish-ready material emerge with minimal ongoing effort. When you think of content this way, your passive income dreams become more achievable, because you've replaced guesswork with a reliable machine that serves your audience while you sleep.

CHOOSING A NICHE AND PLATFORM

Choosing where your content will live and what you'll talk about is the first big design decision for your content engine. The right niche isn't just about passion; it's about sustainability, audience demand, and your capacity to deliver consistently. Likewise, the platform you choose should align with your format strengths and the preferences of your target readers or viewers. Start by asking three questions: what topics am I excited to explore week after week, where do people search for answers in this space, and what format can I sustain without burning out?

A strong niche has three traits: it solves a real problem, it's specific enough to stand out, and it has a reasonable audience size that grows over time. If a niche is too broad, your content can feel generic and hard to differentiate. If it's too narrow, you risk a fragile audience that dries up quickly. The platform you pick should play to your strengths and the rhythm you can sustain. Blogs excel at depth and SEO, newsletters offer direct access to a loyal audience and high engagement, YouTube rewards consistent, well-produced video with strong retention, and social channels reward quick experimentation and real-time conversation.

Think about your strengths as a creator. If you're a good writer who enjoys research, a blog plus a weekly newsletter can be a powerful combination. If you like speaking and storytelling, YouTube or a podcast feed supported by

a newsletter can work well. If you're comfortable with short, frequent updates and like engaging with a community, social posts and micro-content could be your primary channel. Remember that you don't have to be everywhere at once. Start with one primary platform and a single content pillar, then expand as you build confidence and capacity.

A practical way to decide is to map your niche against the platforms in a simple alignment exercise. For each platform, note the content format you can produce consistently, the typical audience size, and the monetization signals you can realistically target. If your page is about practical personal finance for beginners, you might favor a blog with a weekly newsletter and a YouTube channel for short explainers. If your focus is DIY home automation, you may lean toward a YouTube channel complemented by short-form posts on social and a companion blog for detailed walkthroughs. The goal is balance: choose a niche you can own and a platform you enjoy using, then commit to a sustainable cadence that your future self will thank you for.

PROMPT SYSTEMS FOR CONSISTENT OUTPUT

Consistency in AI output comes from well-designed prompt systems rather than relying on a single magical prompt. Think of prompts as reusable templates that encode your rules of thumb: tone, structure, length, and the kind of content you want. A robust prompt system uses multiple layers: a system prompt that sets the overall role, a task prompt that defines the specific output, and a content or style prompt that preserves your voice across outputs. When you assemble prompts this way, you dramatically reduce randomness and drift, and you create a predictable pattern that your audience can recognize and trust.

A typical prompt system includes three core components. The system prompt defines the role you want the AI to play: a clear, helpful guide with a friendly, practical voice suitable for beginners. The task prompt specifies what you want: a blog post, an outline, a video script, or a set of social captions, with constraints on length and structure. The style prompt codifies your voice, examples, and rules about accuracy and sourcing. For example, you might have a prompt that asks for an 800-to-1200-word article with a three-section outline, a concise hook, and a closing takeaway. You could pair it with another prompt that translates that article into five social captions of a specific length and tone, ensuring consistency across channels. This modular approach makes it easy to update one piece of the system without rewriting everything.

Templates are the lifeblood of repeatability. Create a small library of templates for different content formats, such as long-form articles, newsletters, YouTube video scripts, and social posts. Each template should specify the structure and tone, plus placeholders for your inputs. You'll want example prompts that demonstrate how to handle headers, transitions, and calls to action, as well as prompts that enforce fact-checking and sourcing. Version control matters here: label prompts with version numbers, keep a changelog of updates, and test new templates in a controlled way before you roll them out broadly. Finally, build guardrails into your prompts. Ask for sources, require a check against common knowledge, and prompt the AI to flag any claim that seems dubious. This creates a reliable, scalable base you can trust and iterate on.

A note on adaptability: platforms change, audiences evolve, and best practices shift. Treat your prompt library as a living set of guardrails that you revise every few months or after a substantial platform change. When you couple well-designed prompts with a clear editorial voice, your content remains stable and high quality even as the topics you cover expand.

FROM IDEA LIST TO CONTENT CALENDAR

The most powerful way to make your content engine truly autopilot is to turn an open list of ideas into a structured content calendar that guides production for weeks or months ahead. The process begins with a broad brainstorm, but the payoff comes when you cluster ideas into themes, assign them to formats, and slot them into a regular publishing rhythm. The calendar becomes your roadmap, helping you stay relevant, consistent, and scalable while keeping the creative fatigue at bay.

Start with a large pool of ideas generated by you and your AI partner. The ideas come from audience questions, trending topics within your niche, evergreen problems your readers face, and seasonal opportunities. The next step is clustering these ideas into thematic groups. Each cluster becomes a content pillar that supports a cadence of posts across formats. For example, a personal finance channel might cluster around budgeting basics, debt payoff strategies, and simple investing, with each cluster producing a mix of blog posts, newsletters, and short social updates. Clustering helps you see dependencies and makes planning easier.

Once you've defined clusters, you translate them into a cadence. Decide how often you publish per channel, what formats you'll use, and how you'll stagger evergreen versus timely content. A simple approach is to assign one core piece per week per platform, plus supporting micro-content and one call to action that nudges readers toward a revenue opportunity such as a lead magnet or affiliate recommendation. With a calendar in hand, you begin feeding topics into the AI pipeline in advance. The AI drafts outlines, the editors refine the voice, and the scheduling tool pushes posts to publish on the exact days you specify.

Automation tools can help you keep the calendar current without micromanagement. A shared calendar, a topic backlog, and a set of automation rules that queue content for generation are all you need to keep momentum without burning out. In practice, a quarterly planning session is enough to map three to four months of content, with a monthly review to adjust for new opportunities or changing audience needs. The goal is to create a self-repairing loop: new ideas feed the calendar, the calendar feeds content, content drives engagement and insights, and those insights feed new ideas. When your calendar is set, your content engine starts to feel almost autonomous, while still leaving room for your distinctive voice to shine through in every piece.

QUALITY CONTROL: EDITING, FACT-CHECKING, AND ADDING YOUR VOICE

The magic of AI content comes with a caveat: accuracy, trust, and voice don't automatically arrive from the machine. Human oversight remains essential if you want to build credibility and a loyal audience. Quality control should be built into every stage of the workflow, not treated as an afterthought. A practical approach is to insert a human-in-the-loop check after the AI draft but before publication. The draft lands in your editor's lap, where tone, structure, and clarity are polished, and where any factual claims are vetted against reliable sources. This is where your voice becomes visible. AI can generate a clean, well-structured piece, but your stories, examples, and personal observations are what make it resonate.

A simple quality framework starts with clarity and accuracy. Read the draft for obvious errors and for readability. Check that names, dates, figures, and claims have sources or evidence. If the AI quotes or cites studies, verify those citations and link to credible references. Your voice is the texture that turns a good article into a memorable one: insert your experiences, anecdotes, and practical tips, and adjust the language so it feels like you, not a generic template. Accessibility matters too. Ensure there's alt text for images, captions for videos, and plain-language explanations for technical terms. The editor's job is not to rewrite you but to illuminate your perspective and ensure the content serves the audience with integrity.

Guardrails protect you from drift. Maintain a concise editorial style guide that includes rules on attribution, tone, and formatting. Establish a two-pass process: the first pass focuses on structure and accuracy, the second pass refines voice, flow, and engagement. Encourage fact-checking as a habit rather than a chore, and create a lightweight internal glossary for terms and phrases that recur in your content. As you grow more confident, you'll streamline the process: your prompts will often produce drafts that require only minor tweaks, and your voice will become a clear thread through all outputs. The result is content that is reliable, engaging, and unmistakably yours.

CONNECTING CONTENT TO REVENUE: ADS, AFFILIATES, AND LEAD CAPTURE

A content engine only earns money when it translates audience attention into revenue without becoming spammy or manipulative. The monetization plan should feel like a natural extension of the value you already provide. Start with three revenue streams that align with your content and audience. Advertising harnesses the reach of your platform to display relevant ads, sponsorships, or partner placements that fit your readers' interests and your ethical standards. Affiliate marketing invites you to recommend products and services you genuinely trust, with disclosures that preserve transparency and integrity. Lead capture turns readers into an ongoing relationship by offering a valuable incentive—such as an expanded guide, a checklist, or a mini course—in exchange for an email address. Your content engine then becomes a pipeline that nurtures that relationship into future sales and opportunities.

The key is to weave monetization into the content in a way that preserves trust. Ads and sponsors should feel like a natural fit with the topics you cover, not intrusive interruptions. When you recommend products through affiliates, ensure they truly solve a problem for your audience and that you disclose any compensation. Lead magnets should be genuinely useful and aligned with your reader's goals, not gimmicks. The tone should remain educational and helpful, with a consistent emphasis on delivering value before asking for anything in return. This balance is what sustains long-term income rather than producing a short-term spike followed by audience fatigue.

Measurement is how you know you're on the right track. Track engagement metrics such as open rates, time on page, shares, and comments, along with revenue signals like click-through rates on affiliate links, ad revenue per post, and the conversion rate of lead magnets. Use A/B tests for headlines, intros, and calls to action to refine what resonates. Always test ethically: avoid deceptive practices, respect privacy, and provide easy opt-out options. Over time, you'll accrue a portfolio of evergreen content whose value compounds. The engine will generate not just a single post, but a library of credible, utility-driven content that continuously supports your income goals while freeing up your time to pursue new ideas.

FIVE

AI-POWERED DIGITAL PRODUCTS YOU CAN BUILD ONCE AND SELL REPEATEDLY

TYPES OF AI-FRIENDLY DIGITAL PRODUCTS (GUIDES, TEMPLATES, TOOLS, AND MORE)

Digital products designed for passive income thrive when they are both useful and easy to update. AI makes that combination more achievable than ever, especially for nontechnical creators who want scalable outcomes without becoming full-time developers. In this section you'll see a spectrum of product types that AI can help you create once and sell repeatedly, along with how to keep them fresh without endless manual rewriting.

Guides and playbooks form a sturdy base. A well-crafted guide answers a real question with practical steps, a clear pathway, and examples that readers can apply immediately. AI helps by generating a solid outline, drafting readable sections, and drafting variations for different audiences. The core value comes from clarity, actionable steps, and reliable framing. A guide might cover an efficient onboarding process for freelancers, an AI-powered marketing checklist, or a practical approach to automating repetitive tasks in a small business. What keeps these products evergreen is a tight, repeatable structure: problem statement, context, steps, checkpoints, and a simple template that readers can reuse.

Templates and time-saving kits are perhaps the easiest AI projects to own and update. Templates for emails, proposals, contracts, landing pages, and content calendars can be produced in bulk and then personalized in minutes. AI makes it simple to draft the initial versions, adjust tone for different audiences, and generate multiple formats from a single prompt. A template pack becomes more valuable when you include a companion set of instructions and a few example completed templates to show what good looks like. The ongoing work is in tuning the prompts and refreshing content as your target tools or platforms evolve.

Tools and calculators fall into a special category. These are small yet highly usable assets that people will actually keep open on their screen. They can be AI-assisted checklists that adapt to user input, decision trees, or lightweight calculators that estimate time, cost, or impact. The key is to make the tool feel alive without requiring users to learn a new programming language. When AI handles the heavy lifting behind the scenes, you can offer a tool that produces consistent results with minimal user input and extraordinary speed.

Swipe files and discovery libraries provide a ready-made brain to draw from. A swipe file is a curated collection of proven scripts, emails, prompts, and workflows that others can imitate or adapt. AI helps you assemble, summarize, and rewrite materials so they feel original and tailored to a specific audience, then organizes them into an intuitive library. The value is in the speed of deployment and the assurance that successful patterns are already tested.

Mini-courses and script packs are bite-sized education that people can consume quickly. You can assemble a compact course that delivers a handful of lessons, each anchored by a practical assignment. AI accelerates the process by outlining lessons, drafting lecture notes, generating slide prompts, and crafting short quizzes or exercises. The course becomes a repeatable product when you standardize the format, create a landing page that conveys the core outcome, and offer lifetime access or a simple renewal model.

What unites these product types is the ability to create a finished asset with a single strong concept and a repeatable workflow. The real optimization comes from forcing yourself to design around a single audience and a single problem, then letting AI fill in the content and structure. Your job as the creator is to maintain the human layer: a clear promise, credible expertise, and a voice that resonates with your readers or users. As you go, you'll find that AI is not a replacement for judgment and empathy; it is a powerful amplifier that helps you deliver value at scale with less hands-on work.

USING AI TO DRAFT, STRUCTURE, AND POLISH E-BOOKS AND MINI-COURSES

E-books and mini-courses are excellent vehicles for passive income because they can be read or consumed without the creator being present. AI can dramatically shorten the time from idea to finished product while preserving readability, voice, and structure. The secret is to start with a sharp, specific audience and a concrete outcome, then guide the AI with prompts that enforce a usefully narrow scope.

Begin with your audience and the result they want. Frame a clear problem you will solve, then sketch a concise outline that reveals a logical progression from problem to solution. AI excels at turning a simple outline into a first draft, but the real craft comes from your edits and refinements. You can ask the AI to draft one chapter at a time, or draft an entire course module with a defined set of learning objectives and practical exercises. The key is to treat the initial draft as a draft, not the final product, and to actively curate tone, pace, and clarity.

As you draft, you'll want to shape the voice and level of detail. You can instruct AI to write in an approachable, conversational tone or in a professional, concise style. You can demand simpler sentences or richer descriptions. After each draft section, read aloud what AI produced and compare it to real-world examples you respect. Then run a quick audit for consistency, logical flow, and pacing. It helps to insert anchors for the reader—short summaries at the end of sections, practical exercises, and real-world examples—to keep the material grounded and actionable.

Structure is more than organization; it is a promise to the reader about what they will get. Use a consistent framework for each chapter or module: a clear objective, the problem context, the core content delivered in digestible chunks, and a set of practical actions readers can implement. When turning content into a mini-course, convert each section into a lesson with a focused takeaway, a short example, and a quick exercise. You can also create downloadable companions such as checklists, worksheets, and reflection prompts that reinforce learning and give readers a sense of progress.

Editing and polishing take the largest bite of time if you don't plan ahead. Rather than chasing perfect paragraphs, set writing boundaries: define a word count for each section, establish a target reading level, and enforce a consistent structure across chapters. Use AI as a co-editor, asking it to improve clarity, tighten sentences, and reduce repetition. But do not rely on it to judge accuracy or factual claims alone; you should fact-check, verify dates, data, and claims, and add your own expertise where AI's confidence dips.

Finally, plan for format and delivery. Decide whether the product will be delivered as a high-quality PDF, a digital bundle, or a sequence of streaming lessons. Consider offering an audio version or a summary deck that complements the written content. The best AI-assisted books and courses feel like they were written by a thoughtful human who used AI to accelerate the process, not replace the craft. By keeping your eye on the end user's outcomes and iterating on structure, tone, and examples, you can produce E-books and mini-courses that readers will value long after the initial launch.

TEMPLATES, CHECKLISTS, AND SWIPE FILES GENERATED WITH AI

Templates, checklists, and swipe files are some of the most practical digital products you can build because they offer immediate utility and are highly repeatable. When AI handles the heavy lifting of draft creation, you can focus your energy on making sure the resources feel credible, actionable, and tailored to a specific audience. The secret is to design resources that readers can drop into their own workflows with minimal friction and maximal impact.

A template pack can include foundational documents and fill-in forms that people customize for their own situation. Imagine a client onboarding template that guides a freelancer through discovery, scope, and delivery, accompanied by an email sequence that reduces back-and-forth. An AI-assisted template pack can evolve in response to user needs, offering variations for different industries or business sizes. The templates themselves should be accompanied by a short set of usage notes that explain when to use each piece, what to customize, and how to adapt the wording for tone and branding. The value is not in a single perfect document but in a ready-to-go toolkit that saves hours of setup time.

Checklists are another form of high-utility asset. They distill complex processes into a clear, repeatable path. An AI-generated onboarding checklist, for instance, can cover every step from account setup to first deliverable, with optional checks for compliance and security. The accompanying notes should spell out what each step accomplishes and what success looks like. A well-designed checklist is small, but it travels everywhere with the user, becoming a trusted companion that reduces cognitive load and decision fatigue.

Swipe files are the bread and butter of efficiency. They aggregate scripts, prompts, and templates that have stood the test of time in various settings. AI helps you compile, condense, and rewrite items so they feel fresh and aligned with your own brand voice. A swipe file for outreach, for example, can offer a spectrum of email templates and cold-calling prompts that users can tailor to their audience. The real win is in organizing the library with intuitive categories, a search index, and a short explanation of when each piece should be used.

As you create AI-generated templates, checklists, and swipe files, keep a simple principle in mind: utility next to usability. The product should solve a real problem, be easy to adapt, and come with enough guidance that someone who is new to your space can apply it with confidence. You can pair a template with a short instructional video, a few example filled templates, and a one-page quick start guide. Together these additions increase perceived value and reduce the effort required to start using your product immediately.

SIMPLE "MICRO-TOOLS" AND CALCULATORS BUILT WITHOUT CODING

Micro-tools and calculators are small but powerful anchors for a passive income stream. They solve focused problems, require minimal ongoing maintenance, and can be built with no coding knowledge by combining AI with no-code platforms. The core idea is to create something that users will reach for again and again because it helps them make a decision, estimate impact, or save time. With AI you can design these tools to be context-aware, offering personalized outputs based on user inputs while keeping the interface clean and approachable.

A common example is a return-on-investment calculator for AI investments. Users input their current revenue, cost structure, and the scope of AI tooling they're considering, and the tool returns a conservative estimate of payback period, projected revenue lift, and risk notes. Another example is a content ROI calculator that helps a small business measure the potential benefits of creating consistent AI-driven content. You can also build simple pricing calculators for services or product lines, helping a potential client or internal decision maker compare options quickly. The beauty of these tools is that once you've defined the logic and the user inputs, the AI can handle the rest, generating personalized results for every new user.

To build these without code, think of a small architecture: a simple input form, an AI backend that processes the inputs and generates outputs, and a lightweight user interface for display. Notion pages, Airtable bases, or Google Sheets work well as the backbone, while AI prompts drive the analysis behind the scenes. You can deploy a basic web page or a shareable link that runs in the browser, and you can host the resulting tool on your existing platform or a no-friction storefront. The key is to keep the scope tight and the experience smooth. If a user can understand the input they need to provide and can act on the result in a few minutes, you've built a tool that earns its keep.

As you develop micro-tools, consider how you'll maintain them over time. You'll want a process for validating tool relevance, updating AI prompts as models evolve, and refreshing scenarios that demonstrate current market conditions. You can offer a simple license or a small subscription that covers ongoing improvements and new prompts. The best micro-tools feel invisible in their usefulness: they slot into a workflow so naturally that users scarcely notice they are using an AI-powered asset.

PACKAGING, POSITIONING, AND PRICING YOUR AI-ASSISTED PRODUCTS

Packaging is more than a product label; it's a frame that helps potential buyers understand the exact value you're offering. The right packaging makes your AI-assisted assets feel like a coherent system rather than a collection of loose pieces. Start with a clear naming strategy that signals outcome, audience, and scope. A strong name reduces friction, sets expectations, and signals credibility. Beyond the name, think about how you describe the product's outcome in a single sentence that your audience can repeat to themselves. The rest of the packaging comes in the form of a promised journey: what the reader will achieve, how long it will take, and what support they can expect along the way.

Positioning turns packaging into a competitive advantage. Position around the problem you're solving rather than the technology you're using. People don't buy AI because it is AI; they buy it because it saves time, reduces risk, or makes life easier. Position statements should align with real pains and tangible benefits. If your audience is busy professionals, emphasize speed, reliability, and integration with existing workflows. If your audience is solopreneurs, highlight the freedom to scale without hiring more people. In both cases your tone should be confident but grounded in real outcomes, with examples that reflect common scenarios your readers face.

Pricing strategy should reflect the value delivered, the degree of ongoing support, and the willingness of your audience to invest. Consider pricing models that support evergreen sales with occasional updates, such as a one-time purchase plus optional add-ons for updates, or a low-cost monthly plan that includes updates and premium support. A sensible approach is to start with a core price that feels fair for the initial set of assets and then offer tiered extensions that unlock more templates, more robust tools, or faster update cycles. When you price, be explicit about what updates are included and what counts as an upgrade. Clear pricing reduces disputes and builds trust.

Finally, test your packaging in small ways. Launch a pilot with a limited audience to verify the perceived value and adjust your messaging accordingly. Use a simple feedback loop to learn what features readers love, what parts are underutilized, and what extra resources would make the product indispensable. Iteration is inexpensive when you're dealing with digital content, and as you refine your packaging and pricing, you'll find the sweet spot where value, clarity, and ease of use converge.

AUTOMATING DELIVERY, UPDATES, AND CUSTOMER ONBOARDING

The maturity of your AI-assisted products is measured not only by the quality of the asset but by how effortlessly buyers receive and use it. Automation is the engine that turns a one-time purchase into a sustainable income stream. Start with the essentials: a simple payment and delivery flow, a secure file hosting arrangement, and a basic licensing model that protects your work while remaining user-friendly. You can use a straightforward storefront or marketplace where a buyer can purchase, access a download link, and receive a welcome message that sets expectations for updates and support.

Delivery should feel almost invisible to the user. After a successful purchase, the asset should appear in their inbox or be accessible from a dedicated account page within minutes. You can automate access control so only paying customers can retrieve the file, and you can set expiration policies if you offer time-bound access to updates. The moment the buyer receives the asset, you should have a welcome strand of communication that reinforces the intended outcomes, provides quick setup guidance, and invites them to engage with you if they want more help. The goal is to reduce friction and make the user feel guided rather than left to figure things out on their own.

Automating updates is where the AI advantage truly shines. You can schedule periodic refreshes of templates and swipe files to reflect changes in platforms, tools, or best practices. A notification system can alert purchasers when updates are available, and you can offer a convenient upgrade path that keeps everyone on the current version. Customer onboarding should be designed to scale. A short, friendly welcome email coupled with a concise how-to guide and a 2–3 minute walkthrough video can dramatically increase early satisfaction and reduce support inquiries.

Support automation completes the loop. Create a self-service resource library that includes how-to videos, troubleshooting guides, and a searchable FAQ. You can use AI to route common questions to an automated response and escalate only the truly tricky cases to a human. The most sustainable passive income comes from products that feel effortless for users and reliable for you; automation makes it possible to deliver on both fronts. As you implement these systems, design for robustness: monitor for broken delivery links, ensure backups for your templates, and set up clear channels for feedback so you can improve without regressing into chaos. In the end, automation is a promise you make to your future self as much as to your customers: that the business will keep working even while you sleep.

SIX

AFFILIATE MARKETING AND NICHE SITES WITH AI SUPPORT

WHAT AFFILIATE MARKETING REALLY IS

Affiliate marketing is a simple idea with outsized potential: you earn a commission by recommending products or services you believe in, and when your audience makes a purchase through your link, you're rewarded. There is no inventory to manage, no product development to undertake, and no customer service you have to handle yourself. Your role is to connect people who have a problem with a solution that actually helps them, and to do it in a trustworthy, transparent way. The mechanics are straightforward in theory but require thoughtful work in practice. A tracking link registers a sale or a lead, the affiliate network pays you according to the agreed terms, and you repeat this across products and channels to scale your income. The magic comes from building content and audiences that keep returning to your site or newsletter, so every new referral compounds over time.

There are a few common myths worth unpacking. Some people imagine affiliate marketing as a gold mine you can walk into with no effort and instantly print money. In reality, it's more like tending a garden: you plant seeds, water them, watch for pests, and harvest patiently. It takes time to build the trust and traffic that make commissions reliable. Another myth is that you must be a technical wizard with a big marketing machine behind you to succeed. The truth is you don't need to be a software engineer, but you do need clarity about your audience, steady content, and habits that keep you moving forward. The third myth is that any product will do. The best affiliates pick what genuinely helps their readers and aligns with their values. If your audience grows to trust you, they will follow your recommendations, and your recommendations will matter more.

A practical way to think about it is as a two-part cycle: first, you attract and serve an audience with useful content; second, you connect that audience with products that genuinely improve their lives. AI can accelerate both halves. It can help you identify who you're serving, what they search for, and which products solve their real problems. It can draft initial versions of reviews or tutorials, then you bring them to life with your own voice, experience, and ethical disclosures. The real leverage comes from creating assets that keep producing value over months and years, not just weeks.

In terms of workflow, you start with audience understanding. You define who you're helping, what keeps them up at night, and what kind of results they want. Next you select a handful of reputable products that fit those needs and offer credible affiliate programs with fair terms. Then you create content—honest reviews, useful guides, comparison pages, and how-to tutorials—that helps readers decide. You embed affiliate links cleanly and disclose your relationship transparently. Finally you monitor performance, test variations of headlines and calls to action, and refine your approach so it scales without compromising trust. AI shines here by quickly surveying products, organizing consumer sentiment, and drafting initial content outlines, but your voice and integrity are the compass that keeps the ship on course.

If you're wondering whether this model suits you, start with one niche you already care about and publish a few thoughtful pieces over a couple of months. Measure what matters: whether readers click through to your recommended products, whether they convert, and how your content affects long-term engagement. Remember that successful affiliate marketing is less about one spectacular piece of content and more about a steady stream of helpful, up-to-date information that earns trust and proves your recommendations have real value.

CHOOSING ETHICAL, HIGH-VALUE PRODUCTS

The heart of sustainable affiliate marketing is alignment. You're not just chasing the highest commission rate; you're choosing products and programs that genuinely deliver value to your audience. The right products help people solve real problems, fit their budgets, and come with reliable support and transparent terms. A high commission is meaningless if the product consistently underperforms or creates bad customer experiences, because that reflection bounces back on you as the affiliate. Ethical choices start with a clear understanding of your readers' needs and a commitment to honesty in every recommendation.

First, evaluate the problem the product solves. Does it address a pain point your audience actually faces? Is it something people would reasonably pay for, or is it a luxury they might not be ready to invest in? If your niche revolves around time savings, for instance, you want tools that save meaningful minutes or reduce stress, not flashy gadgets with questionable practicality. Price matters, but it's not the only axis. A mid-priced, consistently updated product with strong customer support and a transparent refund policy can outperform a more expensive option with a poor track record. Look at the product's lifecycle: is it updated regularly, does the vendor respond to feedback, and are there long-term improvements visible in user reviews?

Second, scrutinize the affiliate terms themselves. Transparent commission structures, fair payout timelines, and reliable attribution are essential. You want to know precisely when a sale is credited, whether there are performance-based bonuses, and if there are any caps or cookie windows that limit eligibility after a click. While some networks promise generous commissions, a lack of reliable reporting or convoluted terms is a signal to pause. Equally important is the provider's material resources for affiliates. Do they offer helpful banners, product comparisons, or updated feature lists that reflect current reality? Good programs treat affiliates as partners, not afterthoughts.

Third, test the product, or at least its value proposition, before recommending it. If you can, sign up for a trial or a basic account first. Use the product as a customer would and note where it shines and where it falls short. Your firsthand experience is the most credible form of evidence you can offer your readers. If you can't test it directly, lean on independent user reviews and case studies from reputable sources, and look for patterns in the feedback. When you write about the product, tell the truth about both the pros and the cons, and compare it to reasonable alternatives. Honesty isn't just ethical; it's effective. People appreciate practical, balanced guidance that respects their time and their wallets.

Finally, consider the fit with your audience's values. If your readers care about sustainability, for example, highlight vendors with ethical sourcing, green packaging, or donation programs. If privacy and data security matter to them, confirm that the product has robust protections and clear privacy policies. When your recommendations reflect readers' values, your content earns credibility and your affiliate links become trusted pathways to genuine solutions.

AI-ASSISTED NICHE RESEARCH FOR NICHE SITES

Choosing a profitable niche starts with a clear sense of audience needs and an honest assessment of competition. AI can be a powerful partner in this exploration, helping you surface ideas you might not have considered and then vet them quickly. Begin with a broad interest area you care about and then invite AI to brainstorm related subtopics that people search for. The goal is to map a landscape of potential topics that have demand, but not overwhelming competition. AI can generate dozens of candidate topics based on search intent patterns, seasonality, and cross-category relevance, then help you triage them based on several criteria: audience size, willingness to pay, and the speed with which you can monetize.

Once you have a preliminary list, you can use AI to estimate the level of competition by analyzing top ranking pages, their content depth, and the quality of their back-links. You don't need to measure with absolute precision; you're looking for the signal that a topic is defensible enough to build around. A healthy indicator is a topic where you can create superior, easier-to-understand content and where existing top results show room for improvement in areas your voice can complement—practical tutorials, unbiased reviews, and clear, organized data. AI can help you assemble this intelligence quickly, aggregating data from multiple sources and presenting it in a digestible format, but you'll still make the final call based on your gut check about the audience and your own capacity to sustain the effort.

A practical approach is to run through a funnel: define a broad category, extract related subtopics, and then filter those by intent. Look for topics with high commercial relevance, such as product comparisons, how-to guides, troubleshooting, and installation or setup advice. These topics create opportunities for affiliate links within detailed, helpful content. AI can help you generate keyword ideas, long-tail variations, and semantic groupings that map naturally to pillar pages and cluster content. The pillar-and-cluster structure is particularly friendly for AI-assisted workflows because it keeps your site organized and makes it easier for readers to move from general overviews to specific product recommendations.

As you narrow to a final niche, conduct a reality check. Can you produce consistent, high-quality content for at least six to twelve months with the resources you're willing to invest? Do you have access to credible product programs within that space? Are there affiliate programs that offer you a reasonable revenue share and transparent reporting? If the answers point toward yes, you have a practical foundation for building a niche site that uses AI to stay relevant and useful over time.

CREATING COMPARISON GUIDES, REVIEWS, AND TUTORIALS WITH AI SUPPORT

High-quality product content is the backbone of affiliate sites. Readers want clear, practical information they can act on, not marketing puffery. AI can help you brainstorm, draft, and polish content, but the human touch remains essential. Start with a structured approach that keeps comparisons useful and fair. Your pieces should identify who the product is for, what problem it solves, how it performs in real-world use, and how it stacks up against credible alternatives. A good comparison guide covers core criteria such as features, price, ease of use, customer support, and notable quirks. It should also include a transparent verdict that aligns with your audience's priorities, whether that's budget, speed, reliability, or ease of integration into existing workflows.

A helpful workflow begins with gathering reliable product data: official specs, user manuals, pricing, and the vendor's own claims. If possible, test the products or review firsthand accounts to verify the information you present. AI can assemble this data into a cohesive draft and propose an outline for your article. It can draft sections like a concise introduction that frames the problem, a feature-by-feature comparison, and a section that helps readers decide which option is best for different scenarios. After the draft is generated, you tailor the tone to your audience, insert real examples or screenshots sourced with permission, and weave in your personal experiences so the content feels credible and grounded.

Tutorial content adds another layer of value. You can write step-by-step guides on setup, optimization, troubleshooting, and best practices. Each tutorial can explain what to expect, what common mistakes to avoid, and how the product impacts daily routines or workflows. The goal is to provide a practical, no-fluff resource that readers can bookmark and return to. When you publish, accompany your guides with related product links, case studies, and a clear disclosure statement about your affiliate relationship. If you keep your content updated and honest, your readers will see you as a trusted advisor rather than a one-time promoter—and that trust feeds ongoing affiliate commissions over time.

AI can support every phase of this work, from data gathering to draft generation to optimization suggestions. But you should always review for accuracy, verify claims, and inject your personality and concrete examples. This blend of AI efficiency and human judgment creates content that helps readers make informed decisions and keeps your affiliate income steady.

TRAFFIC THE SMART WAY: SEARCH, SOCIAL, EMAIL, AND COMMUNITIES

Traffic is the oxygen of any affiliate site. Without steady streams of visitors, even the best content won't translate into commissions. The smart approach blends search engine visibility with value-driven distribution across social channels, a growing email list, and active participation in relevant communities. Start with evergreen search content that serves long-term intent. Create informative guides, in-depth reviews, and practical how-to posts that answer questions readers actually ask. Optimize for the intent behind the search terms you target: information-seeking queries should lead to how-to content; navigational queries should lead readers to your product comparison pages; transactional inquiries should connect with product reviews and affiliate links in a natural, no-pressure way.

In the social realm, use AI to repurpose your best content into shorter formats that suit each platform. Convert a detailed review into a swipeable carousel for a social feed, extract a few actionable tips for a quick video, or create a thread that teases a more complete guide. The key is to add value rather than simply broadcasting links. Engage with genuine questions, respond to comments, and avoid overt promotional tactics that turn readers away. Across all channels, maintain a consistent voice and a steady cadence. Regular publishing helps your audience learn what to expect from you and when to expect new content.

Email remains one of the most durable channels for affiliate marketing. Building a list allows you to deliver value directly to readers who have already shown interest, making affiliate links more effective. Offer a practical lead magnet, such as a "best-of" product roundup, a practical checklist, or an exclusive how-to guide that ties into your niche. Use AI to draft email sequences that nurture new subscribers, deliver concise product recommendations, and reveal case studies or real-world results. The trick is to balance education with promotion, so your emails feel like assistance rather than advertisements. Finally, identify and participate in relevant communities—forums, Reddit threads, Slack groups, or dedicated hobby sites— where your audience spends time. Contribute meaningfully, answer questions, share insights, and gently reference products only when they genuinely fit the discussion. When you engage with integrity, traffic quality rises, conversion rates improve, and your long-term earnings become more predictable.

The throughline is consistency and usefulness. You don't win with a single viral post; you win with a coherent, multi-channel presence that steadily delivers practical guidance and trustworthy recommendations. AI helps you scale content, tailor distribution, and identify gaps in your coverage, but the real engine is your commitment to helping readers make better purchasing decisions—not merely to click an affiliate link.

AVOIDING SPAMMY TACTICS AND BUILDING LONG-TERM TRUST

The quickest way to derail an affiliate effort is to rely on spammy tactics or dishonest claims. Trust is earned, and once it's damaged it's hard to repair. The antidote to hype is transparency. You should always disclose when a link is affiliate and explain why you're recommending a product. Your disclosure can be concise and clear, but it must be present in every piece of content that includes affiliate links. Readers appreciate honesty, especially when they learn that a recommendation comes with a potential benefit for you. But disclosures alone aren't enough. You need to avoid cramming links into every paragraph, using manipulative headlines, or promising unrealistic results. Honest, value-first content performs much better in the long run.

What sustains trust is accuracy and consistency. Update old content when products change, verify pricing and features regularly, and remove or revise links that no longer point to relevant or high-quality options. When you're comparing products, present verifiable facts rather than sensational claims. If you've had a negative experience with a product, share it and explain how it affected you and your readers, and if possible offer a constructive alternative. Your goal is to be a reliable resource, not a buyer for every item you encounter.

Platform dynamics are another source of risk that you should plan for. Affiliate programs can change terms, networks can alter reporting and attribution, and cookie policies may evolve. Diversification is your hedge. Focus on multiple products and programs across different networks, so you aren't dependent on a single source of income. Invest in your own assets as well: an email list, a loyal audience on a blog or YouTube channel, and a library of evergreen content that doesn't hinge on the success of one campaign. These assets generate stable income even when external platforms shift.

Finally, aspire to a reputation that endures. Speak plainly about price, value, and limitations. If you promise results or outcomes, anchor them in real-world scenarios and your own testing. When readers trust you, your recommendations carry weight. They will share your guides with others, return to your site for updates, and click on your links with confidence. This is how you turn affiliate marketing from a quick hit into a durable, scalable income stream that serves your audience and grows with you over time.

SEVEN

SEMI-PASSIVE SERVICES – PRODUCTIZED OFFERS AND AI-DRIVEN DELIVERY

FROM FREELANCING TO PRODUCTIZED SERVICES

A lot of people start by trading hours for dollars. You answer client emails, you write proposals, you show up for calls, and you deliver work that's unique to each client. It can be rewarding, but it's also exhausting. The moment you add AI into the mix, a different path opens up: packaging your knowledge and skills into repeatable, scalable offerings that feel personalized to the client but are powered by solid processes behind the scenes. This is the heart of productized services. It's not about pretending to be impersonal. It's about creating a service blueprint that consistently delivers value—so you can charge more for less chaos, and you can deliver reliably even when you're away from the keyboard. In practical terms, productized services are defined by a fixed scope, a predictable price, and a delivery timeline. The work is still yours to shape, but the path from inquiry to delivery is standardized enough that you can repeat it for every new client without reinventing the wheel each time. AI helps you hammer out that wheel quickly and with less manual tuning for every single client.

What changes when you shift to productized services is not just the workflow but the mindset. You start with a clear picture of the problem you're solving for a specific type of client. You map every step from onboarding to delivery as a repeatable sequence, and you create templates, prompts, and checklists that let you reproduce it with the same quality each time. The service becomes a system you can hand off to a teammate or an AI agent who follows the same steps and hits the same quality bar. The result is a more predictable revenue stream and greater freedom for you to focus on the highest-value activities—strategy, client relationships, and continual improvement.

Why does this approach pay off? The math changes in your favor. When you price a fixed package, the effective hourly rate often climbs, because you're extracting more value per unit of time and removing the time spent on scoping and negotiation for every new client. The friction of onboarding drops because clients know exactly what they're getting and when. And because the work follows a repeatable process, you can delegate the routine tasks to AI or a junior assistant without risking inconsistent results. With a productized service, you also reduce scope creep. When the deliverables are defined up front, there's less chance of drift into "just one more tweak." This is not a shortcut to laziness; it's a disciplined way to deliver higher quality work faster, with more consistency and less stress.

Let me share a snapshot example. A freelance writer, let's call her Lina, transitions from ad-hoc blog posts to a "Content Starter Pack." The pack includes a 1,000-word pillar post, a 500-word repurposed article, five social captions, and a 1,200-word newsletter seed—all delivered within ten days—with three rounds of edits baked into the price. AI helps draft the pillar post and social captions from a short brief, producing a first pass you can edit in minutes. A straightforward onboarding form collects the client's voice, audience, and goals, and a simple SOP handles the rest: research prompts, outline, draft, edit, and final polish. Lina doesn't stop all custom work, but she reduces it to a handful of repeatable offerings that scale, and she's able to serve more clients without burning out.

If you're reading this, you're probably ready to move toward that same scalable edge. The steps aren't exotic, and you don't need to become a tech whiz to start. You need a clear problem you can solve for a well-defined audience, a tightly scoped package, and a delivery system that can run with AI support. The next sections will guide you through the process of defining that service, building the AI-driven backbone, and turning your practice into something that delivers value while you sleep or take a well-deserved break.

DEFINING A NARROW, REPEATABLE SERVICE

The first rule of productized services is simple: the more specific you are about who you serve and what you deliver, the easier it becomes to systematize. Broad promises invite bespoke work and spiraling scope; narrow promises invite repeatable outcomes. The trick is to pick a problem that's common enough to be scalable but specific enough that you can write a clean, repeatable script for it. Start with the client's pain and work backward to a defined solution. If you can describe the outcome in a single sentence and show how you'll get there in a fixed timeframe, you're on the right track.

To make this concrete, imagine a small business owner who wants an online presence that actually converts visitors into leads. A narrow, repeatable service might be a "Lead-Capture Upgrade" package: a compact audit of the current site, a recommended set of changes, and a delivered asset pack that includes a revised homepage, a lead-capture form, and a lead magnet page. The scope is explicit: one page audit, three deliverables, a two-week timeline, and two rounds of revisions. The price is fixed. And the process is documented so a junior teammate or an AI assistant can replicate it with the same quality.

The service should be designed around the tasks you can reliably perform and the outputs you can consistently produce. Start by listing the recurring tasks you perform for a given client in the last year. Which of those tasks would you always do the same way, regardless of client specifics? Which parts require creative judgment, and how can you support those parts with templates rather than custom improvisation? The goal is to capture the "best practice" steps that, when followed, yield a predictable result. You'll need prompts for AI to generate drafts, checklists to verify quality, and templates for the deliverables that clients expect.

As you sculpt the offer, you'll also need to define clear boundaries. What is included in the base package, and what would constitute an upgrade or add-on? How many rounds of revisions are included, and what constitutes a "rework" that would incur extra time? Your answers shape a transparent value proposition. Remember that your client's perception of value grows when they understand the predictable process behind the result.

A practical way to test your packaging is to pilot the service with a small group of trusted clients or mentors. Invite feedback on the clarity of the scope, the delivery timeline, and the perceived value of the outputs. Use that feedback to refine the language in your sales copy, tighten the scope further if needed, and adjust your pricing to reflect the value you're reliably delivering. The pilot is not a final exam; it's a calibration exercise that helps you lock in a repeatable pattern you can scale.

Narrowing your focus does not mean narrowing your impact. It means choosing a specific problem you can tackle deeply and consistently. With the right scope, the right templates, and a solid AI workflow, you turn your expertise into a repeatable machine that serves clients well, while preserving your energy for growth and new ideas.

AI-DRIVEN RESEARCH, DRAFTS, AND REPETITIVE TASKS

Artificial intelligence shines brightest when it takes over the repetitive, predictable parts of work and leaves you with the space to shape strategy and client relationships. In a productized service, AI can act as a diligent co-pilot that handles research, first drafts, data gathering, and routine revisions. The goal isn't to replace your expertise but to amplify it by removing drudgery and speeding up the path from brief to deliverable.

Consider a service that helps small businesses optimize their content strategy. The client provides a brief and a few constraints. You use AI to perform background research: competitor benchmarks, audience interests, and seasonal trends. AI then produces a draft content plan and a first round of draft pieces aligned with the brand voice. You review, edit lightly, and tailor the tone, add client specifics, and ensure factual accuracy. The final outputs are delivered as a cohesive package ready for publishing. The value you add is not just the text; it's the curation, the voice, and the strategic framing that AI cannot fully own.

A practical workflow begins with a carefully designed intake that captures the client's goals, audience, and preferred formats. You maintain a small library of prompts that reflect your standard methods: prompts to pull market data, prompts to draft outlines, prompts to write headlines, prompts to generate meta descriptions. This library becomes the backbone of your system. You then set up a delivery pipeline where the client's input seeds the AI's generation, and your human review ensures that every output aligns with the client's brand and legal requirements. The outputs move through a defined quality gate: an initial AI draft, a human-driven pass for tone and accuracy, and a final polish.

The balance is critical. AI can speed things up dramatically, but it isn't infallible. Facts must be verified, citations checked, and claims aligned with what you promised. You'll want guardrails in the form of checklists and standard prompts that you always run before delivering anything to a client. Build your SOPs around these steps to ensure consistency, regardless of who is running the process.

When you rely on AI, you also must consider client privacy and data security. Treat the client's inputs as confidential, store drafts in secure systems, and avoid exposing sensitive information through cloud processes that lack proper controls. Make transparency part of your process. Let clients know what AI handles and what you personally verify. That transparency builds trust and reduces the risk of misalignment or warranty claims.

If you want to scale, you will eventually want to layer in more automation. A client inquiry could trigger a smart form that captures the essential data, funnels it into a project workspace, and assigns tasks to your AI prompt library and your QA checklist. The result is a repeatable, AI-assisted workflow that produces consistent outcomes with less manual effort. The combination of AI efficiency and human judgment is what makes a productized service robust, scalable, and ethical.

AI-POWERED SOPS AND CHECKLISTS

Standard Operating Procedures are the unsung heroes of scalable services. They're the rule book for how you execute your offers, and they're what lets your business run while you sleep. The moment you codify each step, you unlock the ability to train someone else, or an AI agent, to perform the work without you having to babysit every detail. The first time you write an SOP, you translate your own tacit know-how into explicit steps, decision criteria, and quality checks. The next time you deliver the service, the SOP acts as the map that keeps you aligned with the standard you've defined.

AI helps you create, revise, and maintain these SOPs with remarkable speed. You can generate draft SOPs from template prompts, populate them with inputs from your service's standard data points, and then refine them to reflect actual practice. The goal is not to create a brittle document that never changes; it's to build a living, breathing system that grows with your business. Each SOP should cover the full run of a service: onboarding, data gathering, AI generation, human review, final delivery, and post-delivery feedback. It should also specify what happens if inputs are missing, if the client asks for a tweak beyond the scope, or if a tool you rely on experiences downtime.

Checklists, closely tied to the SOPs, are where the actual guardrails live. A well-designed checklist converts a process into a reliable sequence of checks that a human or an AI agent can follow. A typical checklist for a productized offer might begin with confirming client inputs, then verifying that all required assets are present, running the AI prompts, reviewing the draft for tone and accuracy, applying brand guidelines, and finally delivering a ready-to-publish asset with client notes and next steps. Checklists are not merely about ticking boxes; they are about ensuring consistency, quality, and a smooth handoff to the client.

You'll want your SOPs to be living documents. Build in regular review cycles, and schedule QA checks as part of the delivery pipeline. When you update an SOP, you should reflect the changes in all dependent checklists, and you should communicate the improvements to any team members or AI operators who rely on them. This is how you achieve true repeatability at scale.

As your business grows, SOPs become more valuable. They enable you to bring in helpers or virtual assistants who can perform the routine work with minimal supervision. They also create a safety net for clients: a predictable experience with a predictable outcome. The better your SOPs and checklists, the more you can rely on AI to carry the journey from inquiry to delivery, while you retain control over the quality and direction of the work.

AUTOMATION FOR BOOKING, ONBOARDING, AND DELIVERABLES

Automation is the nervous system of a semi-passive service. The moment someone expresses interest, an automated sequence can guide them from inquiry to verified appointment, from there into a smooth onboarding flow, and finally into the delivery pipeline. The aim is not to remove the human touch entirely but to remove the repetitive friction that slows you down and reduces your margin. A well-designed automation stack makes it possible to handle more clients without sacrificing responsiveness or quality.

Think of the journey this way: a potential client discovers you, signs up for an available slot, and then enters a structured intake that captures the essentials: business context, goals, audience, preferred format, and any constraints. An automated calendar books the slot and sends a confirmation, followed by an onboarding email sequence that sets expectations, reveals the workflow, and prompts the client to provide any missing information. Your AI prompts can begin drafting the core deliverables as soon as the brief is complete, while you focus on oversight and quality control.

The real leverage comes in the delivery phase. A project workspace, populated with a standard template, becomes the central hub for all client materials. AI can generate the initial drafts, populate the deliverables, and place them into a client portal. You then perform a quick human pass for tone, accuracy, and brand alignment before the final handoff. Automated reminders—about revisions, approvals, and delivery dates—keep the project humming without constant back-and-forth.

Automation also makes billing predictable. An automated invoice can be issued as soon as the delivery date passes, and recurring billing can be arranged for monthly retainers or package renewals. The key is to architect a delivery pipeline that is resilient, with fail-safes for when a tool is temporarily unavailable or when a client submits unusual inputs.

A practical takeaway is to begin with a minimal automation set that covers booking, intake, and a basic deliverable. Once that baseline is reliable, introduce additional automation to the review cycle and the delivery handoff. As you expand, your SOPs and checklists will guide you in adding new automation steps without sacrificing consistency. The result is a system that can handle a growing number of clients with less direct daily involvement from you, while still maintaining high standards of service.

TRANSITIONING TO SCALABLE, SEMI-PASSIVE PACKAGES

The transition from custom work to scalable, semi-passive packages is a journey, not a single leap. It begins with a single productized service that you optimize until it's working smoothly. Once you've proven the concept and the numbers look healthy, you layer in more packages, each with its own narrow scope and automation stack. The goal is to create a portfolio of offerings that share common infrastructure: clear problem statements, repeatable workflows, AI-assisted delivery, robust SOPs, and clean handoffs.

Price discipline matters here. Start with clear value proxies: the time you save the client, the speed of delivery, and the quality consistency you guarantee. Consider value-based pricing where appropriate, but also test fixed-price packages that are easy to sell via simple marketing copy and a straightforward onboarding flow. As you add more offerings, you can cross-sell or upsell where AI enables synergy. A lead-generation package that feeds content for a client's site can be paired with a separate optimization package, and the two can share the same lead capture and onboarding process.

A practical path to scale looks like this. Begin by documenting a base package that you can deliver with minimal customization and a fixed timeframe. Validate it with a handful of clients to gather reliable feedback and metrics. Then codify additional packages that target adjacent but distinct problems, each with its own SOPs and prompts. As you accumulate case studies and testimonials, you'll gain confidence in your value proposition and begin to price for the longer-term outcomes you deliver rather than just the immediate deliverables.

Operationally, the shift to semi-passive work comes with a decision about resource allocation. You may decide to automate the repetitive steps fully and hire a virtual assistant or a junior contractor to handle the client communications, while you maintain ownership of the creative direction and the client relationship. The transition also requires a discipline for ongoing improvement: regularly review performance, track metrics, and refine workflows to keep pain points from creeping back in.

The payoff is real. You'll free up meaningful hours, reduce the emotional load of chasing every new project, and create a business that can ride the wave of AI-assisted productivity. You'll find that scalable, semi-passive packages aren't about removing your role but about evolving it into a more leverageable one. The chapters ahead will help you map your own path—from the first productized service to a sustainable portfolio that grows even when you're not actively trading time for money.

EIGHT

AUTOMATING SMALL BUSINESS OPERATIONS FOR ONGOING INCOME

FINDING TIME LEAKS

Small online businesses often feel like a rhythm you can't quite hear until you pause and listen. The truth is that most success comes from keeping a steady beat rather than hitting a few big notes. The way to regain control is to map your current workflow, stretch out the parts that slow you down, and identify opportunities to automate without changing the heart of your business. This starts with a simple, practical audit you can actually do without a tech degree.

Begin by choosing a representative period—two weeks is plenty for most small operations. During that time, document what happens from the moment a prospective customer first hears about you to the moment money changes hands, and then beyond: onboarding, follow-up, and support. You're not chasing every minute; you're looking for patterns. How many times does a task repeat in a day, a week, or a month? What tasks take longer than you'd like, and which ones feel necessary but draining? Record the tools you touch, the data you move, and the touch points where sentience and judgment feel required. You'll typically notice a few core flows dominate: customer inquiries, order processing, onboarding, follow-up, and reporting. If a process involves a lot of manual copying, data entry, or back-and-forth emails, that's usually a sign a candidate for automation.

As you begin to map, your aim is to create a simple picture of cause and effect. You'll trace an inquiry to a sale, a sale to onboarding, onboarding to ongoing engagement, and so on. Bottlenecks reveal themselves as moments of friction: duplicate data entry, multiple hand-offs between tools, repetitive responses to the same questions, or constant status checks that pull you away from higher-value work. Don't overcomplicate this. The map should be easily understood by you and anyone who helps with the business, not a maze of diagrams.

With the map in hand, assess value and effort. High-value tasks are those that move a customer forward or increase revenue, while effort captures the time and cognitive energy required to complete them. Look for automation candidates among repetitive, rules-based activities that don't require nuanced human judgment. For example, if you spend hours each week sending the same set of emails, updating the same spreadsheets, or compiling reports, those are prime targets for automation. The idea isn't to replace you but to replace the drudgery with smart systems that do the legwork while you focus on higher-value decisions and creative work.

As you identify candidates, set a modest pilot plan. Choose one or two processes that represent a meaningful chunk of your time and test a lightweight automation approach. The goal is to prove what's possible with a minimal investment of time and money, then scale what works. During the pilot, track outcomes with the same clarity you used for the audit: time saved, error reduction, and the impact on customer experience. If the pilot shows a clear win, document the new process so you can replicate it elsewhere. If not, refine, or shift to another candidate. The point of this exercise is to create reliable, repeatable flows that don't require you to become a technologist—instead, you become a systems thinker who leverages AI to do the heavy lifting.

Finally, plan your next steps. By the end of the audit you should have a short, actionable list of automation opportunities and a realistic timeline for testing them. You'll know which bottlenecks to tackle first and how much time you'll gain back to reinvest in growth or in rest. The objective isn't speed for speed's sake, but steadiness: more predictable revenue, less stress, and a business that can run a little more on autopilot while you decide where to invest your newfound time and energy.

AI FOR CUSTOMER SUPPORT

Great customer support isn't magic; it's structure, clarity, and the right balance between automation and human touch. In a small business, AI can take care of the repeatable questions and create a scaffold so your human team can handle the rest with genuine care. The vision is a support experience that feels fast, helpful, and human, even when a machine is doing the heavy lifting.

Start with your knowledge base. Gather all the questions you most often hear from customers and document clear, concise answers. When you can, augment those answers with short, how-to steps, screenshots, and links to resources. This living library becomes the brain that powers any AI assistant you deploy. The better your knowledge base, the less your customers feel they are talking to a robot and the more they feel understood and guided.

Next, introduce an AI-assisted FAQ system that can answer common questions instantly. The aim isn't to replace people but to reduce the idle time customers face when waiting for a reply. A well-trained bot can handle routine asks about shipping times, returns, account access, and product compatibility. When the question lands outside its comfort zone, the system should gracefully hand off to a human agent with the full context of the conversation so the transition feels seamless rather than jarring.

Chatbots are most effective when they are transparent about their role. A short preface like, "I'm here to help with quick questions. If I can't resolve it, I'll connect you to a human agent," can set the right expectations. And the handoff should be frictionless: the customer's chat history, the issue summary, and key data points should be visible to the human agent so the responder doesn't have to start over.

Help docs should be treated as dynamic assets. Every time you get a support ticket that reveals a gap in the documentation, update the article or create a new one. This continuous improvement approach reduces repeat inquiries over time and improves the quality of every future reply. When you train your AI, you should build in guardrails for tone, accuracy, and privacy. The goal is to deliver prompt, useful responses while avoiding overconfidence or the misrepresentation of capabilities.

Measurement matters. Track metrics that matter to your business: response time, first contact resolution, customer satisfaction scores, and escalation rate. Set expectations for your team: a clear service level goal that feels reasonable for a small operation. If your metrics drift, adjust the system. Perhaps you need a more robust knowledge base, or a different balance between AI and human support. The key is to make customer support faster, more consistent, and more scalable without sacrificing empathy and personal connection.

EVERGREEN MARKETING THAT RUNS

Marketing in a small business can consume endless energy if you try to chase every trend. The antidote is a thoughtfully designed machine: evergreen email sequences and social posts that educate, nurture, and convert with minimal daily effort. The aim is not to crank out content endlessly but to craft a few core messages with durable relevance and let AI handle the rest—drafting, scheduling, and responding to audience signals.

Begin with the customer journey. A welcome series for new subscribers sets the tone, shares your story, and points toward a resource that helps them solve a concrete problem. From there, build a sequence that teaches, builds trust, and introduces a low-friction offer. The sequences should be long enough to show value but short enough to keep the message consistent and non-intrusive. With evergreen content, you aren't chasing newcomers every day—you're guiding a long-running audience through a well-lit path to a decision.

AI shines in this space by drafting language that aligns with your brand voice and goals. It can turn a webinar transcript into a blog post, a short explainer video script into bite-sized social posts, or a long-form newsletter into multiple email variants for testing. The key is to maintain a human touch: approve the core ideas, adjust the tone to suit your audience, and customize the opening and closing messages so they feel personal rather than automated.

A scheduling backbone is essential for consistency. A simple calendar that maps when to publish, what to publish, and where to publish creates a reliable rhythm. evergreen sequences should live in a central hub, so if a legal requirement changes or a product update occurs, you only fix one source instead of chasing multiple channels. When AI generates content, keep a light editorial hand. Review the outputs in batches rather than in real time to preserve quality and relevance.

Creative curation also matters. Reposting best-performing content with updated angles keeps your channels fresh without burning you out. Reuse older posts by repackaging them into new formats—an introductory post can become a short video, a longer article, or an infographic. Always respect privacy and permission—do not repurpose content that violates someone's rights or uses data beyond what you've disclosed. The core idea is to convert your existing knowledge into a steady stream of touchpoints that convert without running you ragged.

Finally, measure and adjust. Track open rates, click-through rates, and engagement benchmarks. Let data guide you toward what to amplify and what to retire. When a campaign shows durable performance, you can scale it by widening distribution, tweaking headlines, or refining the offer. The goal is a sustainable marketing engine that remains effective as your business grows and as AI capabilities evolve.

BETTER DECISIONS WITH LESS MANUAL WORK

Numbers don't lie, but they do need a translator. AI can translate your data into clear, actionable insights so you can make confident choices without drowning in spreadsheets. The idea is to replace hours of manual digging with concise, automated summaries that highlight what matters most and prompt you toward the next action.

Think of your analytics as a living cockpit. You pull data from orders, payments, customer interactions, and marketing channels, and a lightweight AI layer processes it into a narrative that's easy to understand at a glance. It might read like a weekly briefing that points out anomalies, confirms trends, and suggests guardrails: when revenue dips by a certain percentage, when a product line becomes less profitable, or when your cost of customer acquisition crosses a threshold that warrants a pivot.

A practical starting point is to define a small set of core metrics that reflect the health of your business. Revenue and profit are obvious, but add engagement signals like active customers, repeat buyers, and funnel progression. AI can summarize weekly changes and explain why they happened. For instance, it might note that a spike in refunds coincided with a policy change or that a marketing campaign is driving more low-quality leads than high-quality ones. The goal is not to prove the AI's infallibility but to give you a trusted ally that highlights what needs your attention.

Pair the summaries with simple dashboards. You don't need a fancy BI tool to get value; a clean overview is enough when data is current and well-organized. The dashboards should pull from familiar data sources such as your CRM, payment processor, and email marketing platform. The automation layer should deliver a short narrative each week with a couple of recommended actions. If you prefer more detail, you can click through to a deeper report, but the primary objective is a crisp, actionable overview.

As you rely more on AI for analytics, remember the boundaries. Data quality matters more than quantity. If inputs are inconsistent, even the best AI will generate noise. Establish simple data hygiene practices: consistent labeling, regular cleanup, and a clear process for correcting mistakes. And stay mindful of privacy and compliance. You're dealing with real people and their data, so ensure your AI use respects consent and data protection rules. The aim is to empower decision-making with clarity and speed, not to replace human judgement with blind automation. With reliable summaries at your fingertips, you can move from reactive firefighting to deliberate, strategic operations.

In the end, AI-enabled analytics should feel like a thoughtful co-pilot: there to alert you, summarize, and propose options, while you retain final say over strategy and values.

BACK-OFFICE RESILIENCE: INVOICES, PROPOSALS, AND DOCS

The back office isn't glamorous, but it is the backbone of a scalable business. When this part of your operation hums, you free yourself to focus on growth, not paperwork. The key is to create a disciplined, templates-first approach that reduces repetitive work, speeds processes, and preserves professionalism across every client interaction.

Start with templates that cover your most frequent tasks: proposals, invoices, contracts, and onboarding documents. A well-crafted template is a contract you never have to rewrite from scratch. It should be clear, professional, and adaptable enough to handle a range of clients without losing its structure. As you build these templates, keep a consistent tone and branding. This consistency is not about rigidity; it's about trust and reliability. When you automate, you should still feel confident that every document you send represents your business accurately and ethically.

Automation shines in recurring administrative tasks. Invoices should generate automatically when a project reaches a milestone or a service period ends. Reminders can be scheduled ahead of due dates, and late notices should be polite but clear. A digital signature capability makes it feasible for clients to approve proposals and sign contracts without back-and-forth delays. The aim is to shorten the cycle from agreement to execution, so you can move on to delivering value sooner rather than chasing documents.

Proposals deserve special attention. A strong template that captures scope, milestones, pricing, timelines, and terms helps you convert faster and reduce underbidding or scope creep. When a client provides a brief, you should be able to generate a polished proposal quickly, then customize a few key details while preserving the underlying structure. This is where AI can be most helpful: it can draft initial versions based on your patterns, which you then review and tailor. The more you lean into templates and automation, the more consistent your client experience becomes and the more predictable your revenue looks.

Document creation flows should be transparent and efficient. From client intake forms to ongoing project updates, use a centralized repository so everyone knows where things live and what stage they're in. Naming conventions, storage structure, and access controls matter. When a file is updated, the system should automatically tag it with version numbers and dates so you avoid confusion or miscommunication. The overarching objective is to reduce friction, protect data, and ensure every document is a professional reflection of your brand. With reliable admin processes in place, you'll have more time to invest in value-added work and new income opportunities.

TURNING FREED-UP TIME INTO NEW INCOME STREAMS

The whole point of automating operations is not simply to save time; it's to create space for growth, experimentation, and higher-value work. Freed-up hours are capital you can reinvest in new income streams that scale beyond your personal output. The most practical strategy is to pick one or two new offerings that can leverage your existing expertise and the automation you've built, then test them with low risk and high clarity.

One powerful approach is to productize a service. Take a recurring client workflow you've already automated— onboarding, deliverables, reporting—and package it as a repeatable service with clear pricing, deliverables, and timelines. Because you've automated the heavy lifting, you can offer this service to more clients without requiring linear increases in your own effort. The first step is to define the scope so it feels personalized but remains repeatable. The second step is to set up a predictable delivery cadence using your existing AI-assisted processes, so customers get consistent results without you trading time for money at every turn.

Another avenue is to convert your knowledge into a digital product. A short course, a series of templates, or a niche toolkit can be created once and sold repeatedly. AI can help you draft the content, assemble the materials, and format the package for delivery, but your role remains essential: you validate the problem, ensure the solution is practical, and provide the human touch that makes the product trustworthy. Start with a minimal viable product, then gather feedback from early buyers and refine before you scale.

Diversification doesn't require a leap into new markets. It's a series of small, deliberate experiments that align with your strengths and the automations you've set up. Each experiment should have a simple test: a defined audience, a fixed price, and a short window to evaluate performance. If the experiment lingers in limbo, it's a signal to either pivot or park it for later. The mindset here is sustainable growth rather than impulsive hustle. Build systems that can run with limited supervision and that gently push you toward more stable, passive income. The bigger your automation moat, the easier it becomes to expand into adjacent ideas and protect your business from shocks, seasonality, or platform changes.

NINE

BUILDING YOUR FIRST AI INCOME SYSTEM – A STEP-BY-STEP BLUEPRINT

CHOOSING YOUR STARTER PROJECT

The first principle of building an AI income system is choosing the right starting point. Imagine you're steering a small boat rather than a cargo ship. You want something light, sturdy, and capable of moving you forward even when you're not at the helm. That means a starter project should be low in complexity, deliver a clear payoff, and fit your current skills or the interests you already have. When you pick the right project, you create momentum. When you pick something too big or risky, you stall before you begin.

Start by asking two simple questions. What problem can I solve that people are already willing to pay for, and how quickly can I deliver a credible solution? The broader the market, the more attractive the opportunity, but the bigger the project tends to be. Look instead for a sweet spot: a problem with a straightforward solution and a short path from idea to value. You don't have to reinvent the wheel. You're looking for a frictionless entry that yields a tangible payoff within weeks, not months.

Think in concrete terms about what you can offer that leverages AI without requiring deep technical skills. One promising approach is to bundle AI into a simple asset or service that can be delivered with a repeatable, repeatable process. For example, you could package a weekly AI-assisted content kit—a batch of blog post outlines, social media captions, and a few SEO-friendly headlines—that you sell for a small recurring fee or a one-time price. A different route is an automated assessment or checklist that adds value quickly, such as an AI-generated resume optimization guide or a niche market research brief tailored to a specific audience. These examples share a common trait: they're easy to produce once and then scale with the same workflow.

To evaluate ideas, give each one a quick, practical score on four dimensions: demand, ease of delivery, the potential price point, and the size of the market you can realistically reach. A high score in all four isn't always possible, so you'll make tradeoffs. The goal is to land on something you can complete in a few weeks with a reliable output that customers understand and value. If you can't imagine a clear, near-term payoff, step back and choose a different idea.

Once you've narrowed to a couple of possibilities, pick the simplest one that promises a real payoff. Don't over-think the design or the exact feature set. Your aim is to create a tiny but robust system that proves your concept and earns you your first money online. The first project is not your final one; it's your learning exercise that shows you what works and what doesn't in your actual environment. Your assignment is to brainstorm three starter ideas that fit the criteria above, then choose the most straightforward option that offers a tangible payoff within a few weeks.

As you begin, remember that ethics and sustainability aren't optional add-ons. You want a model that respects user privacy, delivers real value, and can operate without constant maintenance. The right starter project respects boundaries, avoids hype, and provides a foundation you can scale responsibly over time.

PLANNING THE SYSTEM: MAPPING INPUTS, PROCESSES, AND OUTPUTS

Before you touch a tool or write a single prompt, you plan the system. A clear system map is a mental blueprint you can translate into actions later. The map helps you see how data flows from the moment it enters the door to the moment value reaches your customer. It also reveals dependencies, potential bottlenecks, and where human oversight is still needed. By starting with inputs, processes, and outputs, you build a framework that stays intact as you add tools and automate more steps later.

Your system has three core dimensions. Inputs are everything you feed into the system. They include the topic or niche you're serving, the audience you're addressing, any existing assets you'll reuse, and the data you'll collect during the process. In a simple AI content system, inputs might be a topic brief, a keyword list, and a target word count. Processes are what happens to those inputs. They are the prompts you send to the AI, the checks you perform, and the small edits a human would do. Outputs are the final products delivered to customers—whether that's a ready-to-publish article, a downloadable asset, or a personalized report.

To make this concrete, imagine you're building a weekly content bundle for small business owners. The inputs include topics the audience cares about, a tone guide, and a handful of target keywords. The process starts with an AI-generated outline, followed by a full draft, with a quick human edit to ensure accuracy and voice. The final output is a blog post plus a batch of social media posts that can be scheduled automatically. A simple feedback loop checks engagement metrics and click-through rates, feeding insights back into future topics and prompts. This is your system map in motion.

A practical way to articulate your plan is to sketch a small diagram or write a short paragraph describing the flow.

You don't need fancy software; a whiteboard or a notebook works. The key is to name each stage, identify who or what performs it, and decide how you'll measure success at that stage. Define a lightweight feedback mechanism early. It could be a quick customer check-in after delivery or a simple metric like completion time or quality score. Early feedback is priceless because it guides adjustments long before things go off the rails.

Finally, anticipate constraints. Budget matters, so design the system to run under a modest monthly cost. Data privacy and ethics matter, so decide what data you'll collect, how you'll store it, and how you'll handle user consent. You don't need a full-scale data governance plan yet, but you should know where your data sits and who has access to it. A realistic map acknowledges limitations and sets boundaries that keep you on track.

Your exercise for this section is to articulate your system map in a paragraph or two. Name the inputs you'll start with, describe the core processing steps, and define the final output you'll deliver to customers. Add a sentence about the feedback you'll collect and how you'll use it to improve. This exercise keeps your eyes on the prize while you're still choosing tools and prompts. A clear plan today prevents chaos tomorrow, and this clarity is the seed of reliability.

SETTING UP YOUR AI WORKFLOWS AND AUTOMATIONS

With a clear map in hand, you're ready to assemble the pieces. The aim here is to connect simple tools into a functioning pipeline that can operate with minimal daily input from you. You'll set up the core automations, define your prompts precisely, and build the checks that keep output quality high. The beauty of this stage is that you don't need to become a coder to create real, scalable automation. No-code and low-code options let you wire things together with visual interfaces and intuitive settings.

Begin by choosing your primary workflow engine. A dependable approach is to pick a single AI service to generate content, another tool for editing or quality checks, and a scheduler that decides when outputs are created and published. The exact tools aren't as important as how you connect them and how well you understand the prompts you feed into the system. Your prompts should be concise and purposeful. A good prompt for an article outline might be:

"Create a detailed outline for a 1,200-word blog post about [topic], tailored to [audience], with three subheadings and three bullet points for each subheading."

For the draft stage, a prompt could be:

"Write a clear, engaging draft in a friendly, authoritative tone, targeting readers who are new to [topic], including an introduction, five sections, and a concise conclusion."

The edits and quality checks are equally important. You can implement a lightweight human-in-the-loop system: a quick skim to catch obvious factual errors, a style check to ensure voice consistency, and a plagiarism or repetition check to keep outputs unique. These steps protect you and your audience from sloppy results and potential reputation risk.

Automation is a living system. Start with a simple, repeatable loop and iterate. If the draft is too long, trim it and tighten the language. If engagement is low, test a different hook or angle. If the output feels off-brand, adjust the tone guide and the prompts accordingly. A small but well-tuned loop compounds quickly, delivering steady results without turning you into a content factory.

Safety and ethics should be at the forefront. You're not just aiming for speed; you're aiming for accuracy, fairness, and respect for your audience. Build in checks for factual consistency, credit where due, and transparent disclosures if AI is a significant part of the process. If a topic touches on sensitive information, implement guardrails or expert review to avoid misrepresentation or harm.

Finally, test the end-to-end flow before you go live. Run a few pilot outputs, publish them to a private audience, and collect feedback. Note any friction points—the steps that consistently slow you down or degrade quality—and refine them. The objective is a smooth, dependable pipeline that you could leave running while you're away from your desk for days at a time.

As you set up, document your configuration. A short notes file that explains which tools you're using, how they're connected, and the prompts you've settled on becomes priceless when you scale. It reduces cognitive load and makes onboarding easier if you decide to expand or bring in a partner later. Your job is not to build the perfect system on day one but to construct a sturdy, maintainable pipeline you can trust and improve.

CREATING AND LAUNCHING A MINIMUM VIABLE OFFER OR ASSET

This section is about turning your well-planned system into something customers can actually buy. The MVP concept here is simple: deliver the smallest viable asset or service that provides recognizable value and can be produced quickly, with room to improve after real-world use. An MVP asset isn't a final product; it's a tested proof of concept that proves people will pay for what you're offering and gives you priceless real-world feedback.

Think of your MVP as a clean, tangible deliverable that sits neatly within your system map. It could be a ready-to-use digital asset—like a set of AI-generated templates, checklists, or a mini-course—that a customer can download and implement with minimal effort. It could also be a productized service: an AI-assisted evaluation or optimization report that you deliver on a monthly basis. The key is that the asset or service is concrete, repeatable, and scalable with a single workflow.

A concrete example helps. Suppose your starter project is an AI-assisted content package for small business blogs. Your MVP could be a weekly bundle that includes a 1,200-word guide, five social media posts, and a short email newsletter, all tailored to a specific niche. The asset is delivered as a downloadable package with a simple, clear explanation of how to use it. The price point is modest to keep the buy-in low and the risk small. Behind the scenes, your system generates the content each week using your established prompts, then automatically packages and delivers it to the customer.

Launching the MVP requires a lean workflow. Create a basic landing page that clearly communicates the value and the exact deliverables. Offer a simple checkout process and immediate delivery—no long forms, no labyrinthine options. Announce the MVP to your network, in communities you've identified as ideal customers, and through a few paid ads if your budget allows. The feedback you gather in the first two to four weeks is more valuable than a hundred optimistic guesses. Listen for what customers praise and what they skip, and use those signals to refine your asset and your messaging.

Pricing should reflect the value you deliver and the reality of a slow, early-stage market. You're not aiming for maximum profit on day one; you're aiming for a sensible balance that invites trial and reduces barriers to purchase. A common early tactic is to offer a soft launch discount or an introductory bundle to encourage early adopters and collect testimonials. Keep the offer simple and transparent: what's included, how delivery happens, and what a customer can expect after purchase. If you can automate 70–80 percent of the process, you're in a sweet spot where the MVP can scale with little incremental effort.

Your MVP is your teaching tool as much as your revenue generator. It demonstrates the viability of your idea, anchors your pricing, and highlights the gaps you'll fix in the next iteration. The goal for this section is to produce an asset or service you can put in front of real users within a short window, capture meaningful feedback, and use that feedback to drive the next cycle of improvements.

SIMPLE LAUNCH PLAN: TRAFFIC, FEEDBACK, AND FIRST CUSTOMERS

With your MVP in hand, you're ready to give it a public debut. The launch plan isn't about a big splash; it's about a lean, repeatable process that brings you your first customers and a steady stream of insights. The aim is to attract the right people, not everyone, and to convert interest into paying customers with minimal friction. A simple launch plan focuses on clarity, credibility, and a fast feedback loop.

Begin by identifying where your ideal customers spend time online. Choose one or two channels where you'll be active and consistent. It could be a niche forum, a small business community on a social platform, or an email newsletter list you already own. The idea is to meet people where they are and invite them to try your MVP. Your outreach should emphasize a clear, tangible outcome: what the customer will gain and how easy it is to get started. Use real-world language and avoid hype. Your message should answer the question, in plain terms, what problem are you solving and why it matters.

Content is your first, most reliable driver of interest. Create a lightweight content plan that explains the value of your MVP through useful, practical examples. The content should not be about you; it should demonstrate how your asset makes a real difference in someone's day. The AI can help here too—generate blog posts, short video scripts, or social media captions that illustrate the exact benefits and outcomes your buyers will experience. The content should invite conversation and encourage people to take the next step: visit the landing page, learn more, and make a purchase.

Conversations with potential customers are your gold. Invite questions, offer a no-friction trial, or provide a money-back guarantee if your product isn't a fit after a short window. Capture contact information and permission to follow up. You'll need it later for testimonials, case studies, and future launches. As you accumulate feedback, you'll learn which features resonate, which messages move people to buy, and which channels offer the best return on effort. Your aim is not a perfect launch but a reliable one—a repeatable, learnable process that scales.

Finally, set a simple, measurable goal for the first launch window. It might be "five paying customers and a handful of feedback interviews" or "ten sign-ups and two testimonials." The exact numbers don't matter as much as the discipline. Track what brought people in, what turned them into customers, and what turned them away. This data becomes the engine for your next cycle of improvements.

In this section, you're building the bridge from idea to real customers with a plan you can repeat. The focus is on credibility, speed, and learning. A successful launch isn't a single event; it's a process you can streamline, refine, and replicate as you add more assets and expand your AI-powered offerings.

REVIEWING, FIXING, AND OPTIMIZING YOUR SYSTEM AFTER 30 DAYS

Thirty days is enough time to learn a great deal from your first AI-powered income system. You'll have data, customer feedback, and a clearer sense of what works and what doesn't. The question now is how to translate that knowledge into meaningful improvements without getting overwhelmed by complexity. Start with a calm, structured review. Look at three things: performance, quality, and viability over time. Performance measures how much output your system produces, how reliably it runs, and how much you're spending. Quality assesses the value delivered to customers—the relevance of the outputs, the usefulness of the assets, and the consistency of your delivery. Viability is about the long game: does this project have legs? Can you scale it without sacrificing quality or stealing too much time from your life?

Begin with a lightweight audit of your workflow. Identify bottlenecks that slow you down or degrade output. Perhaps the prompts need refinement, or the checks catch more errors than you expect. Maybe the delivery process could be made smoother, or the pricing adjusted to reflect the value and costs more accurately. You don't fix everything at once. Choose one or two high-impact areas and iterate. Small, deliberate changes compound into real improvements over days and weeks.

Consider the numbers with a practical eye. Calculate the direct costs of running the system, including AI usage, hosting, and any third-party tools. Subtract this from revenue to understand your gross margin. Then estimate the time you spend maintaining the system. If that time is creeping up, you've got a sign that automation needs to be stronger or tasks should be further delegated to AI or outsourced effort. If your margins are healthy, look for ways to scale: add new markets, extend the asset with slight variations, or create a second MVP that mirrors the first but targets a different audience.

A crucial aspect of this review is customer feedback. Read every testimonial, query, and complaint as a data point. What do customers love? What do they wish for? What features do they miss? Use these insights to inform your next cycle of improvements. The path from here is to refine the MVP, expand its reach, and then replicate the process with a new asset or service. Your long-term goal is a portfolio of AI-powered assets and services that operate with minimal daily attention, freeing you to pursue new ideas and opportunities.

Finally, document what you've learned. Create a compact playbook for your system: what works, what to watch for, and how to adjust prompts and workflows as the market shifts. Recipe-style notes help you scale without losing consistency. The more you write down now, the faster you'll be able to replicate success when you launch your next project. This 30-day review isn't a one-off check; it's the first chapter in a habit of continual improvement that will keep your income system resilient and adaptable over time.

TEN

RISK MANAGEMENT, ETHICS, AND STAYING AHEAD OF CHANGE

COMMON RISKS: PLATFORM DEPENDENCY AND ALGORITHM SHIFTS

Real-world risk rarely wears a neon sign. It hides in the quiet places where your income flows from one piece of software, one platform, or one algorithm. If your revenue rests on a single tool or a single channel, a policy update, a pricing change, or a tweak in an algorithm can ripple through every part of your plan. It's not about fear; it's about foresight. The first quiet risk is platform dependency. You build a business on a tool that automates your content, handles your delivery, or drives traffic. If that tool shifts its terms, freezes access, or deprecates a feature you rely on, your entire workflow can stall. The second risk is policy changes. Platforms update rules, sometimes silently, and the consequences hit your bottom line long after the change takes effect. A new rule about data usage, a stricter guideline for monetization, or tighter requirements for disclosure can suddenly turn a previously compliant setup into a gray area. The third risk, algorithm shifts, is the ever-present tide of discovery. When search rankings and feed visibility swing, yesterday's best workflows can become today's dead zones. Your income flows from patterns and reputations built on an algorithm's preferences, and those preferences can move without warning.

Hedging against these risks starts with diversification and deliberate design. Start by creating assets that are not tightly coupled to any single platform. An email list, a blog, or a scalable digital product can continue to generate value even if a platform disappears or changes its terms. Build workflows that can be ported across tools, and keep your data exportable. Treat your core assets as portable capital rather than lock-in arrangements. To guard against policy changes, document your compliance rituals. Maintain a living checklist that maps your processes to current terms of service and data-use policies. A quick audit every quarter can reveal gaps before they become costly. For algorithm shifts, design your workflows so small changes cause only small disruptions. Version your outputs, create templates, and keep a library of assets that can be re-routed to alternative channels with minimal friction.

Another practical hedge is cash flow discipline. Maintain a reserve that covers two to three months of essential operating costs. When you're in the growth phase, reinvest thoughtfully rather than chasing every shiny new feature. A core principle is to test in small, controlled ways. If you experiment with a new AI tool, do it on a small fraction of your traffic or a single product line first. That way you learn without risking the rest of your income stream. Finally, cultivate a mindset of ongoing risk monitoring. Set up a lightweight rhythm: a monthly review of platform terms, an alert system for policy announcements, and a quarterly stress test of your revenue mix. This isn't paranoia; it's the discipline of resilience. When change comes—and it will—your business should bend, not break.

In practice, resilience looks like a portfolio of small, diversified winnings rather than a few big bets on a single lever. You'll sleep easier knowing your income isn't hostage to a single page on a single site. You'll feel freer to innovate, because you know you have safe paths to reroute if something goes awry. The aim is not to eliminate risk but to illuminate it, manage it, and keep moving forward with confidence.

LEGAL AND COMPLIANCE BASICS: COPYRIGHT, DISCLOSURES, AND DATA USE

Whenever you create and sell or publish with AI, you step into a legal space that looks technical but operates on a few simple principles. You don't need to become a lawyer to stay on the right side of the rules; you just need a practical framework you can apply consistently. The three pillars you'll lean on here are ownership and licensing, disclosure and transparency, and data use and privacy.

First, ownership and licensing. The big question is: who owns the outputs and what rights do you have to monetize them? The safest starting point is to assume that you own the content you create, including AI-assisted content, unless a tool's terms state otherwise. Some platforms explicitly grant you broad commercial rights to outputs, while others reserve certain rights or require attribution. The most important move is to read the terms of service of every tool you depend on and to document your understanding. When you publish an asset—whether it's a digital product, a blog post, or a course—check that all components are properly licensed. This includes stock images, music, videos, and excerpts that may have copyright constraints. When in doubt, opt for assets with explicit commercial licenses or create originals rather than guessing.

Second, disclosures and transparency. The ethical and, increasingly, legal expectation is that you let people know when AI contributed to the creation or curation of content. You don't need to reveal every step of your model's reasoning, but you should inform customers if AI tools generated or heavily assisted the output. For digital products and online services, a brief disclosure statement inside the product or on your sales page can protect you and build trust. The point is clarity, not apology. If you're using AI to compile or summarize user data, say so and describe what data you collected and how it was used.

Third, data use and privacy. Respecting user data isn't optional in today's world; it's foundational. Treat data with care, minimize what you collect, and be explicit about consent. If your process involves training or fine-tuning models with customer information, you should obtain clear permission and provide an option to opt out. Ensure your privacy practices align with applicable regulations, such as general data protection standards or local equivalents. This doesn't have to be complicated. A simple privacy notice, a clear data retention policy, and secure data handling practices go a long way. If you collect email addresses, payment details, or behavioral data for analytics, outline what you store, how you'll use it, and how long you'll keep it.

Finally, build a lightweight compliance habit into your routine. Create a monthly mini-audit that checks licensing on all assets, confirms the truth of disclosures, and reviews how data is managed. You don't need to hire a law firm to stay safe; you need a repeatable, sane process you actually follow. By treating legality as a habit rather than an afterthought, you protect your business and your customers, and you set a standard for ethical practice that others will respect and follow.

SPOTTING SCAMS AND 'TOO GOOD TO BE TRUE' AI OFFERS

The AI space is crowded with promises that glitter enough to distract even careful readers. The problem isn't that everything is insincere; the problem is that some offers are engineered to exploit impatience, fear of missing out, or a lack of experience. The red flags are often subtle, but they're worth learning to spot. If something promises effortless riches in a matter of days, with minimal risk and sophisticated verk of hype, pause. When a program asks you to invest a large sum upfront for a guaranteed return, that's a strong signal to investigate more deeply rather than sign on the line. If the testimonials feel manufactured or repetitive, if the funnel relies on pressure to purchase immediately, or if the offer lacks open detail about how results are achieved, those are red flags. A credible opportunity invites questions, provides verifiable data, and offers a test period that doesn't require you to commit all your capital.

Another telltale sign is a vague or proprietary "secret sauce." If the essential method is hidden behind a password-protected module or a private mastermind group, you may be stepping into a black box. Realistic programs explain the mechanics in plain language and show you examples of actual workflows rather than promising mystical shortcuts. Beware offers that seed fear or fomo. If the messaging relies on an imminent collapse of the current market or insists that you must act now to avoid losing out forever, you should slow down and assess more carefully. The absence of a clear, step-by-step plan is another warning: it's hard to deliver a verifiable outcome when you can't articulate the process.

How should you assess a potential opportunity? Start with your own due diligence. Check who is behind the offer, review independent feedback from third parties, and look for a transparent outline of the method, the required inputs, and expected outputs. Demand a sample of work before you buy in. Request a minimal, low-cost pilot that allows you to test the core idea with real data and real users. If the offer requires you to share sensitive information or payment details before you have validated results, treat it as a warning rather than a savings opportunity. Keep a mental checklist in your head: Is there a clear path from action to result? Are the costs proportional to the intended outcome? Can you realistically measure progress and adjust if the plan isn't delivering?

Finally, protect yourself with skepticism tempered by curiosity. Treat every offer as a hypothesis you need to test, not a fixed truth you must accept. Start small, set measurable milestones, and build in review points that force you to pause and validate. The aim is not cynicism but discernment. With the right guardrails, you can explore new AI tools and opportunities without becoming a casualty of aggressive marketing or hype-filled claims. You're looking for evidence, repeatability, and a transparent process—not magical shortcuts.

ETHICAL USE OF AI: TRANSPARENCY, ATTRIBUTION, AND PROTECTING USERS

Ethics in AI isn't a luxury feature you add after you've built something. It's the backbone of sustainable, trust-worthy income. When you bake transparency into your process, you create a stronger foundation for long-term relationships with customers and collaborators. Start by clearly communicating where AI is involved in your product or service. If you use AI to generate content, summarize data, or recommend products, tell your users. A simple, upfront notice that explains the role of AI can reduce confusion and build confidence. The goal is not to hide the tool; it's to help people understand how the tool affects their experience.

Attribution matters, too. If AI is used to draw on someone else's content or if you license data or prompts from a third party, give credit where it's due. This isn't just about legal compliance; it's about professional integrity. When you publish content that's AI-assisted, consider including an attribution line such as *"AI-assisted drafting"* or a brief note about the role of AI in shaping the output. It's a small gesture that respects creators and manages expectations. You'll also want to be mindful of content that could mislead users. If AI-generated content is presented as human-made or if it could misrepresent a product's capabilities, you risk harming users and eroding trust. Your policy should include guardrails that prevent misrepresentation and ensure accuracy. When possible, pair AI output with human review or verification for critical information.

Protecting users means protecting data and ensuring safety. Design with privacy in mind from the start. Collect only what you need, store it securely, and be explicit about how data is used. If your system processes sensitive information, implement privacy by design and consider data minimization as a default. Deploy robust security practices and communicate them clearly to users. In addition, be mindful of the potential for bias in AI outputs. If your tools can reflect or amplify biases, address them openly and provide mechanisms for users to report concerns or request alternative options. The ethical approach is proactive, not reactive. It builds trust, reduces risk, and often improves your product's quality.

Finally, ethics is a discipline of continuous improvement. You should regularly assess your practices about transparency, attribution, and user protection. Schedule time to review what you publish, how you describe AI's role, and whether your safeguards meet evolving expectations and legal standards. By treating ethics as a living framework rather than a checkbox, you'll create a more resilient, reputable business that can withstand scrutiny and grow with integrity.

DIVERSIFYING YOUR INCOME STREAMS OVER TIME

A sustainable AI-powered income looks less like a single fountain and more like a garden with multiple, nourishing streams. The advantage of diversification is resilience. If one stream hits a rough patch or a platform shifts its winds, the others continue to provide air for growth. A prudent path starts with a small, solid core and gradually expands into related, self-sustaining channels. Think of your core as a scalable asset—something you can replicate, optimize, and reuse. This might be an AI-assisted digital product, an evergreen content engine, or a semi-passive service with repeatable processes. Once that core is stable, you can add complementary streams that rely on similar skills that you already possess. These could be affiliate marketing driven by AI-crafted content, a niche site that earns through ads and partnerships, or a service offering that is productized and automated to deliver consistent results.

As you diversify, preserve synergy rather than chasing novelty. Streams should feed one another. A successful content engine can become the backbone for affiliate income, and your AI-driven digital products can supply recurring revenue that fuels marketing for other ventures. Diversification also means geographic and language expansion opportunities. If your audience exists in one region, consider how your system could be adapted to another audience with localized content and compliance requirements. The goal is to create a portfolio with over-lapping strengths so that each element reinforces the others rather than competing for attention.

A practical approach is phased expansion. Start with your strongest, lowest-friction stream and use profits to vali-date a second stream that complements your first. The second should be a natural extension—sharing audiences, leveraging the same distribution channels, or using the same list for cross-promotion. When it's time to add a third stream, ensure you can maintain quality and support. Don't scale for the sake of scale; scale for resilience. The more your income streams are coherently connected, the easier it becomes to optimize, automate, and maintain them over time. Remember, diversification isn't about chasing every trend. It's about building a portfolio that can endure changes in markets, platforms, and consumer preferences while still helping you sleep better at night.

Ultimately, diversifying is a mindset as much as a strategy. It requires patience, careful experimentation, and the humility to prune underperforming assets. If a stream proves too resource-intensive for its return, it's reasonable to sunset it and reallocate. The best portfolios aren't static; they evolve as your skills grow, as tools improve, and as customer needs shift. Stay curious, but stay disciplined. The longer you maintain a balanced mix of income sources, the more sustainable your lifetime of passive AI income becomes.

CONTINUOUS LEARNING WITHOUT OVERWHELM: A SIMPLE HABIT-BASED APPROACH

Learning is a lifelong advantage in the AI era, but it can also become a trap for distraction and burnout. The solution isn't to study nonstop; it's to adopt a simple, repeatable rhythm that keeps you current without stealing your time. The core idea is to replace passive browsing with purposeful habit stacking: pick a few reliable sources, schedule short, consistent learning sessions, and immediately apply what you've learned to your projects. Start with a lightweight blueprint: one 15-20 minute daily micro-learning block on a fixed schedule, one 30-60 minute weekly review of your progress, and a monthly deep dive into a single, practical area that will move one of your income streams forward. If you build this into your calendar, it becomes automatic rather than aspirational.

The first pillar is curation. Choose a small, trusted set of sources. These can include official product blogs, reputable AI research notes written for non-experts, and practical case studies that show how other people used AI to automate real tasks. Avoid the urge to chase every new app or platform. Your time is valuable, and depth matters more than breadth when you're starting. The second pillar is practical application. Every time you learn something new, you test it on a real project. Whether it's refining a workflow, improving a template, or testing a small feature, you should see a tangible impact within days. The testing itself is the learning. The third pillar is reflection. Schedule a recurring time to review what worked, what didn't, and why. If a new tool saved you two hours this week, document what you did and how you might reuse the approach. If a tactic didn't yield results, write down what you would change next time.

To prevent overwhelm, combine learning with execution. Use a two-phase approach: learn, then ship. The learning phase is intentionally compact. The shipping phase asks you to implement a concrete, measurable improvement within a defined window. This keeps you moving forward rather than spiraling into research for its own sake. You'll also want to build a lightweight risk-management lens into your learning habit. When you're tempted to try something radical, schedule a review milestone to assess the potential upside against the time and resource costs. A good rule of thumb is: if you can't see a clear path to a tangible outcome within two weeks, don't invest heavily right now.

Finally, remember that sustainable progress comes from consistency, not intensity. The small daily wins compound over time into real, durable capability. Your aim is to build a personal operating system that stays relevant as tools evolve and markets shift. With a simple, habit-based approach to learning, you'll keep your skills fresh and your income streams resilient, without losing your balance in the process.

DESIGNING A SUSTAINABLE, AI-POWERED INCOME LIFE

LOOKING BACK AND WHY IT MATTERS

If you've reached this point, you've already started a quiet revolution in how you earn. You've moved from waiting for perfect opportunities to creating reliable, AI-powered systems that work for you every day. The ideas in this book aren't about chasing hype or chasing overnight fame. They're about practical, sustainable leverage—using AI to amplify what you already bring to the table, whether that's a knack for writing, a skill in design, a talent for drawing traffic, or a gift for organizing complex tasks into simple steps.

Over the chapters you've read, you learned to pair curiosity with restraint. You learned to validate ideas before you invest time or money. You discovered that the most powerful AI is not a silver bullet but a set of tools that, when used with discipline, compound your results over months and years. You explored the range of models —from content engines that publish with minimal hands-on work to productized services that scale through repeatable processes. You saw how AI can automate routine tasks, draft the first version of a project, or crunch data you could never sort manually. The goal throughout has been to keep you in the driver's seat while granting your business the speed and consistency that were once possible only to large teams.

A crucial takeaway is this: automation should complement your strengths, not erase them. Your unique perspective— your voice, your judgment, your design sense, your ethics —remains the heart of every successful AI system. When you blend human insight with machine capability, you create a product, a service, or a platform that feels human, not robotic. The chapters urged you to be wary of "set it and forget it" fantasies and to design with ethics and transparency in mind. You learned to ask hard questions about data usage, privacy, and the potential for bias. You practiced partial automation that preserves control, so you're never at the mercy of a single tool or supplier.

Reflect for a moment on how your mindset has shifted. You've moved from "I can't possibly do this" to "I can test, iterate, and improve." You've built the habit of starting small—testing a single narrative, a tiny product, or a short automation sprint—and letting feedback steer the next steps. You've forgone perfect plans in favor of a rolling, adaptable approach. And you've recognized that real, sustainable income isn't a magic trick; it's a system of small, dependable bets that accumulate over time. As you close this part of the journey, remember why you started: to gain more freedom, to protect your time, to build something that can continue to grow even when you're not actively directing it.

In the pages ahead, you'll translate this reflection into an actionable road map. But first, acknowledge the progress you've already made. The simple, repeatable systems you've learned to create can be scaled, refined, and diversified. You don't need to reinvent the wheel every month; you need to keep the wheel turning—and gradually make it smarter, faster, and more aligned with your life goals.

CRAFTING YOUR 6- TO 12-MONTH AI INCOME ROADMAP

A roadmap is not a rigid timetable; it's a living plan that evolves as you learn. The goal here is clarity: what starts as a single, well-defined project can become a family of income streams, all powered by AI and designed to require less direct labor over time. Start with a single, high-probability project that fits your skills and your aspirations, then expand in a measured way as you gain confidence and proof-of-concept results. The structure below is a guide you can adapt, not a destiny you must follow to the letter.

Begin by choosing a primary project that leverages your strengths and satisfies a real need. It might be a digital product that can be created once and sold repeatedly, a content engine that grows audience and affiliate revenue, or a semi-passive service that scales with automation. Define what success looks like in concrete terms: monthly revenue target, number of clients or customers served, hours saved per week, or the size of your audience. Attach a learning goal to each milestone: what AI tool or technique will you master, what compliance or ethical consideration must be reviewed, and what quality standard you'll hold for every deliverable.

A practical way to structure the 6- to 12-month plan is to map three horizons. In the first horizon, the focus is validation and learning. You'll run a short, low-risk test of the core idea, measure the impact, and decide whether to proceed. In the second horizon, you scale the winning approach, automate a larger portion of the workflow, and build a repeatable process you can replicate. In the third horizon, you diversify—add a complementary project or two that shares infrastructure, so you can weather shifts in demand and platform changes without starting from scratch.

To keep your roadmap actionable, attach dates that feel ambitious yet realistic. For each milestone, specify the output you'll produce, the metrics you'll monitor, and the person responsible for the task—namely you. Include a learning budget. AI tools change quickly, and staying current is essential, but don't over-invest in tools you haven't validated. Reserve time for review and adjustment. A monthly check-in is enough to keep momentum without turning progress into busywork.

Think about risk in practical terms. What could derail your plan, and how will you minimize the damage? You might plan for partial automation failures, platform policy changes, or shifts in audience behavior. Build contingencies into your roadmap so you can pivot with minimal stress, not panic. Finally, embed a simple ethical guardrail. Before you deploy a new automation, ask: does this respect user privacy? Is it truthful and transparent about its AI involvement? Will this scale while preserving the quality and humanity of your work? When these questions are baked in from the start, the roadmap becomes not just a route to income but a framework for responsible growth.

As you write your own roadmap, imagine the months ahead as a series of small, steady wins. Each milestone should feel within reach, but each one should also stretch you a little—enough to teach you something new and move you closer to your larger life goals. You'll begin by validating a single idea, then you'll graduate to a second project once the first proves itself. The momentum you build will be the real asset: a disciplined process you can rinse and repeat with higher confidence, more skill, and less friction.

BALANCING AUTOMATION, CREATIVITY, AND HUMAN CONNECTION

Automation without soul is hollow. The most durable income systems honor the human touch—the voice that makes your content feel real, the judgment that keeps your products honest, and the relationships that turn one-time buyers into lifelong supporters. The real power of AI is its ability to free time for what matters most: your creativity, your relationships, and your decision-making. When you strike that balance, you don't simply chase efficiency; you cultivate resonance.

Think of your AI setup as a toolkit designed to enhance your strengths, not replace them. Use automation to handle repetitive tasks: scheduling posts, drafting initial drafts, compiling data, or routing inquiries. Then bring your distinctive voice, your sense of humor, your strategic thinking, and your human capacity for empathy to the work that truly benefits from it. The goal is to keep your work human while letting machines handle the drudgery. This blend is what sustains momentum over months, not just weeks.

In practice, this balance looks like a workflow where AI drafts a blog post, you edit for tone, weave in a personal anecdote, and add a concluding insight that only you could provide. AI can summarize customer feedback into actionable insights, but it's your decision about which insight deserves attention, and how you'll respond. AI can run analytics, but your interpretation guides the next action. AI can generate multiple design options, yet your eye for aesthetics determines the final choice. In every case, you stay in the driver's seat, guiding and shaping the output so that it aligns with your values and your audience's expectations.

To preserve human connection, build rituals that keep your audience at the center. Reply to comments and messages with genuine warmth. Share behind-the-scenes glimpses of your process to reinforce trust. Use storytelling to frame your content and products, letting your experiences color the value you deliver. Remember that transparency is a competitive edge in a crowded market: let people know when you use AI, how it benefits them, and where human oversight remains essential. When you lead with authenticity, automation becomes a force for deeper, more meaningful engagement rather than a cold machine in the background.

This section isn't a manifesto against technology; it's a reminder that your most sustainable income comes from what only you can contribute. The best AI systems multiply your strengths and preserve your unique perspective. They also create space for you to explore new ideas, collaborate with others, and fine-tune what truly resonates with your audience. The result is income that not only grows but also stays aligned with who you are and the life you want to live.

AVOIDING BURNOUT: SIMPLE SYSTEMS FOR TIME, ENERGY, AND FOCUS

Sustainable income isn't built on heroic, all-night sprint sessions. It grows from rhythms that honor your energy, protect your attention, and respect your boundaries. The simplest way to achieve this is to implement lean, repeatable systems that can operate with minimal daily intervention. When you automate the right steps, you don't just gain hours—you gain mental clarity, predictability, and better decision-making. The path here is practical: design routines that you can actually keep, even on Busy Tuesday mornings or when a curveball arrives in your schedule.

Start with a disciplined but forgiving planning habit. Set a single, clear objective for the week and outline the smallest steps that will move you toward it. Use time blocks to protect your focus. Reserve a portion of your week for maintenance—checking analytics, updating content, refreshing data sources—so you're not perpetually chasing the next fire. When you combine automation with a reliable schedule, you create a cadence that becomes almost self-perpetuating.

The first lever you should pull is your workflow efficiency. Map a simple end-to-end process for your core project: from idea to publish, from customer message to resolved inquiry, from product revision to market launch. Identify the tasks that can be automated, the points where human input is essential, and the handoffs that cause bottlenecks. Then compress or eliminate unnecessary steps. Even small reductions in cognitive load can add up to meaningful gains in time and energy.

Second, protect your energy through smart tool use and boundaries. Limit the number of different AI tools you depend on, especially tools that don't integrate well with your workflow. Too many options create decision fatigue. Build a minimal stack that covers your needs well and is easy to maintain. Schedule breaks and protect them. The brain isn't designed to sustain peak performance for long stretches; it needs rest, a moment to reset, and a chance to return with fresh perspective.

Third, safeguard your wellbeing as a business asset. Sleep quality, regular movement, and time away from screens are not luxuries; they're productivity multipliers. The book's guidance has always prioritized steady progress over heroic effort. You don't need to sacrifice your health to grow your income. If anything, a healthy pace is the surest way to protect long-term gains. Build a culture of honest review—if something feels off, if a system isn't delivering, if you're consistently exhausted, pause, reassess, and adjust rather than push through pain.

Finally, stay alert to scams and platform changes. AI tooling evolves quickly, and some models or marketplaces shift their policies. Create a simple safety net: diversify income streams, document processes, and retain ownership of core assets whenever possible. The most durable systems can weather the ups and downs of tech platforms because they're flexible, modular, and well-documented. By focusing on sustainable, low-friction workflows, you'll keep your energy high and your results steady.

MEASURING SUCCESS BEYOND JUST MONEY: FREEDOM, SKILLS, AND OPTIONS

Money is a convenient measure, but it's only a single lens on your progress. The true value of AI-powered income is the freedom it creates—the freedom to choose when you work, where you work, and how you live. It's the freedom to experiment with new ideas, to reinvest in learning, and to respond to life's demands without sacrificing your financial stability. To capture this broader impact, broaden your metrics beyond revenue. Track how much time you reclaim each week, how many recurring processes you've automated, and how your capacity to serve your audience or clients has grown.

Skill growth is another essential metric. Each project you complete, each automation you implement, and each new tool you master compounds your capabilities. In practical terms, you should note not just what you built but what you learned along the way. How did you improve your writing, marketing, or product design? How did your decisions improve the customer experience? When you look back, you'll realize that skill development compounds faster than a single revenue milestone, yielding long-term leverage that compounds over years.

A third dimension is options—the career and lifestyle choices that become feasible when your income becomes more predictable and automated. You may choose to negotiate more flexible hours with an employer, transition into consulting with a scalable service model, or launch a second or third income stream that complements your existing one. The very act of building systems creates options you didn't have before: the option to pause, to pivot, to invest in a new venture, or to retire earlier than you planned. Those options are priceless because they are the true measure of freedom.

Ethics should be part of your measurements as well. If you're relying on customer data, you should be tracking consent, privacy, and transparency. If you're partnering with other businesses, you should assess alignment with your values and the potential reputational impact. The goal is not to chase growth at any cost but to grow in a way that feels aligned with who you are and what you want for the future. When your metrics reflect freedom, skill, and responsible growth, you'll have a more resilient and satisfying business that stands the test of time.

FINAL ENCOURAGEMENT: START SMALL, ITERATE, AND LET THE SYSTEMS WORK

If there's one core message to carry forward, it's this: start where you are, with what you have, and let the systems do the heavy lifting over time. The most powerful success stories in this book didn't begin with a grand plan; they began with a single, deliberate step that was designed to learn, refine, and scale. You don't need to wait for perfect conditions, and you don't need to mortgage your future to chase a dream. You need a reliable, repeatable process that can run with minimal supervision while you keep shaping it with your lived experience and your evolving goals.

So pick one small project today. Map out a 30-, 60-, and 90-day plan. Decide what you will produce, which AI tools you will learn, and how you will measure progress. Make sure you have a safety net in place—backup plans for data, a way to pause if a system isn't working, and clear boundaries so you don't burn out in the process. Then begin. Not perfectly, not instantly, but again and again until the loop becomes second nature. Every cycle will teach you something new and push you closer to a life where your income is reliable, scalable, and aligned with the life you want to live.

As you embark on this final stretch, remember that success is not a single moment of breakthrough. It's a continuous practice of improvement. Your capacity to design and maintain AI-powered systems will compound with time, just as the outcomes you seek compound with effort. Give yourself permission to learn slowly, to test boldly, and to adjust gently. The world of AI-powered income is not a festival of sudden wins; it's a garden that rewards patience, stewardship, and careful cultivation. The systems you build will grow with you. They will adapt to new tools, new audiences, and new opportunities. And over years, they will quietly, stubbornly, reliably support the life you set out to create.

www.ingramcontent.com/pod-product-compliance
Lightning Source LLC
Chambersburg PA
CBHW071413210326
41597CB00020B/3488